Grizzlies In
Their Backyard

BETH DAY

VANCOUVER • VICTORIA • CALGARY

Heritage House Publishing Company Ltd.
#108 – 17665 66A Ave.
Surrey, BC V3S 2A7
www.heritagehouse.ca

Library and Archives Canada Cataloguing in Publication

Romulo, Beth Day, 1924-
    Grizzlies in their backyard

ISBN 978-1-895811-16-2

    1. Stanton, Jim. 2. Stanton, Laurette. 3. Knight Inlet (B.C.)—Biography. I.
Title.

FC3845.K53Z49 1994   971.1'1   C94-910037-4
F1089.K53R65 1994

Printed in Canada

Heritage House acknowledges the financial support for its publishing program from
the Government of Canada through the Book Publishing Industry Development
Program (BPIDP), Canada Council for the Arts, and the British Columbia Arts
Council.

The Canada Council | Le Conseil des Arts
for the Arts | du Canada

BRITISH COLUMBIA
ARTS COUNCIL
Supported by the Province of British Columbia

Covers: Grizzly bears were as much a part of the Stantons' everyday life as the
spectacular scenery surrounding them at the head of Knight Inlet in B.C.'s Coast
Mountains. Photos by Art Wolfe/Image Finders.

*This book has been produced on 100% post-consumer recycled paper, processed
chlorine free and printed with vegetable-based dyes.*

Dedication

To the memory of my father, Ralph Feagles,
who first suggested this book to me,
and to his friend and hunting partner, Dr. J.W. Bowers,
who saw to it that the Stantons and I finally met.

Contents

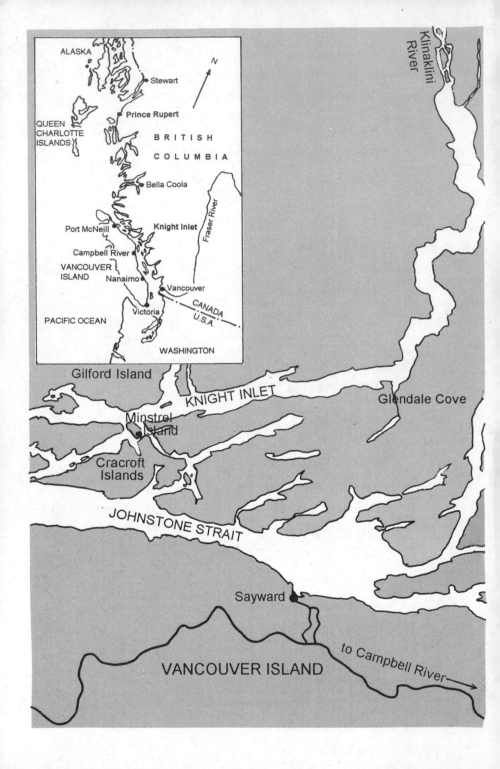

Preface

The grizzly is the largest game beast on the North American continent and the most powerful carnivore in the world today. When standing erect, the adult is from five to eight feet in height. It weighs from three hundred to twelve hundred pounds. The word "grizzly" seems to have an evil connotation. While Noah Webster most likely never met one, his dictionary warns us that the grizzly's "strength and ugly temper make it very dangerous when brought to bay."

Many people have seen grizzlies in a zoo. Thousands of Natives have killed grizzlies simply because they were afraid of the awesome creatures. Hundreds of big-game hunters have shot grizzlies for the trophy pelts. But few people have deliberately and intimately lived among grizzlies for half a lifetime as Jim and Laurette Stanton did. And not only did they have grizzlies as neighbors; they also had three grizzly cubs as their pets.

Jim was personally acquainted with grizzlies. He knew their habits, hideouts, and personalities. For twenty years he ran a trapline through unexplored forests in which he encountered at least a half-dozen grizzlies every day. Jim had actually fought grizzlies. But in his many years in the woods he killed just five of them—all in defense of life or property.

For over thirty years this wiry little woodsman and his slender, brown-eyed wife, Laurette, lived, by choice, in one

of the most remote regions of the North American continent: a rugged land of 13,000-foot peaks, giant glaciers, and inaccessible forests.

To the Stantons, the grizzlies were neighbors, just like the wild deer, the mountain goat, the mink, weasel, and marten who shared their isolated life in the north woods. They not only lived at peace with these wild animals; they shared their food with them and even made some of them pets. Laurette, especially, befriended everything from little pink pigs to grizzlies. While Jim trapped and killed for a modest livelihood, Laurette shuddered at the thought of hurting an animal, either friend or foe.

Why did the Stantons give up civilization? Neither Laurette nor Jim was born in the woods. Their final destination came about—as so many fateful things do—from a few casual fishing trips, and it ended in a lifetime of living as close to nature as man can get until it becomes his final resting place. They were able to succeed in this venture by learning how to wrest a living from the untamed forest: by trapping, fishing, guiding, and handlogging. Together they built their own home, learned the ways of keeping and preparing food, and found by grim experience how to live— often without money and without doctors or any communication with the outside world— through the eternal frozen silence of the long winters in the north woods.

Why did they go and did they find what they were looking for? Their story will tell you.

For every gain there must be a sacrifice. The Stantons did not find peace; perhaps there is no peace anywhere. In the deep woods and the snowbound mountains the survival of the fittest prevails. Even though Jim was far in the forest, trapping mink and marten, their livelihood—their very existence—was affected by the raids of voracious timber wolves and, back in civilization, the rise and fall of the fur market. Perhaps a whole winter's work would go for naught. There might be no money,

no food, no medicine, nothing between them and eternity but their love and faith in themselves.

But the Stantons did find contentment and happiness. They found it in working, trapping, hunting, and literally fighting to keep alive. When a man and a woman are alone in the wilderness, there is a close feeling of oneness that cannot be experienced elsewhere. She cannot live without him; and he is utterly lost without her.

When you are in the forest, embraced by majestic mountains, you can place your hand upon the earth and feel the pulse of nature. You can awaken a thousand mornings and, opening the cabin door, feast your eyes and your soul on breathtaking beauty. And as the years pass and your sight dims, the view will always be clear because no eyeglasses are needed for the memory.

This book is about grizzlies. But it is also about a man and a woman: Jim Stanton, who had to trap and shoot wild animals because that was his trade, and Laurette Stanton, who never carried a gun and never harmed a living thing—a kindly, compassionate woman who suffered every time her man had to kill. They broke away from civilization and went into the great north woods of British Columbia to wrest their living from nature. It starts a long time ago …

Publisher's Note

This photo shows Jim and Laurette Stanton and author Beth Day outside the Stantons' house on Knight Inlet. Beth had heard stories about the Stantons all her life from her father, who regularly visited Jim and Laurette. When Beth was 32 she fulfilled her lifelong dream of meeting them. Her weeks with the adventurous couple led to this delightful book, first published in 1956. It became a bestseller and was later condensed by *Reader's Digest*.

At the time the book was published, the Stantons were in their seventies. A few years later, in 1961, Laurette died in the coastal community of Alert Bay. Afterward, Jim tried to settle in Vancouver, but he kept returning to his beloved Knight Inlet. He died in 1978.

Two Crazy People

One warm, windy day in late June, 1919, a small double-ended rowboat, powered by a 2½-horsepower kicker engine, threaded its way among the maze of channels and islands in Queen Charlotte Strait, which separates Vancouver Island from the mountainous western coast of British Columbia. At the tiller was Jim Stanton, a short, wiry, auburn-haired young man with a tip-tilted Scotch nose and observant blue eyes, etched by squint-lines.

Beside him sat his boyishly slender wife, Laurette, brown hair pushed under an old fishing cap, widely spaced brown eyes fixed eagerly on the rolling emerald water which parted before their boat.

Along with complete fishing equipment for casting and trolling, they carried a balloon-silk tent so that they could camp ashore. Jim had his 30-30 rifle and plenty of ammunition. Their staple foods were packed in watertight tins; they had canned heat, and a lazy board to lean against so they could eat their meals aboard while anchored in a sheltered cove.

Suddenly two channels appeared before them; Jim let go of the rudder, leaving the boat to choose its own course. Putting an arm around her, he pulled Laurette down with him behind the spray hood which was battened over the fore two-thirds of their boat.

The small craft hesitated momentarily where the two channels met, shuddered in the cross currents, and then, leaving Seymour Narrows, the main steam channel to Alaska, it swerved right and plunged toward the high blue mountains ahead.

"That's wild country up there," Jim said, pointing. "Are you game?"

The water had quieted and Laurette stood up, flinging out her arms. "It's glorious!"

"Grizzly country, maybe."

"You and your grizzlies! But Jim," she said thoughtfully, "I have a feeling that we'll find what we're looking for here."

"There'll be hardship, too," he reminded her. "We haven't much money, you know."

"If we'd waited until we did, we'd still be back in Seattle. We took a chance, and I'm glad!"

"A mighty big chance, dear." Jim laid a hand on the rudder again, steadying it. "I've got to find some way to make a living; and we need a roof and a fire before winter sets in."

"Meanwhile," Laurette said contentedly, "we can fish and dream."

The decision to leave their comfortable city apartment for a precarious existence in the wilderness had not been made impulsively. Until 1919, when Jim was thirty-four, he was the the owner of a successful garage business in Seattle. But beneath the surface of this prosaic existence, there burned in each of them an intense love for mountains and forests. They took every opportunity to flee the city and roam the woods, and all the time Jim nurtured a deep desire to live in grizzly country and become intimately acquainted with the strange and, to him, fascinating beasts. As a youngster he had seen a few grizzlies from far off, and listened to many "tall tales" about them.

He had never forgotten the years spent in the woods with his foster father, Evan Evenson, the only real parent Jim ever had. Jim's own father, a railroad construction engineer, had been killed in a work accident before Jim was born; and his mother had died in childbirth. There were few orphan homes at the turn of the century, and Jim was passed around casually from family to family. He learned to saw wood and clean cattle barns on farms. He washed endless stacks of dishes in town houses. A crippling bout with rheumatic fever, followed by a year in bed, had left him undersized, with a "runt's" terrifying inferiority complex. There were sporadic sessions in school, where he didn't get along with either teacher or classmates. In his own words, he was "a mean little devil, always itching for a fight."

Evan Evenson offered to take the unruly boy when he was nine years old. Jim was wiry and tough, and the Norwegian bachelor, who trapped each winter in the forests of northern Washington, needed help on his trap line. Each fall Evan bought old horses for $2.50 apiece and packed up into the mountains. When the freeze came, he shot the horses and used them for bait. He would trap marten until after Christmas, then start cruising for black bear; in the early spring he trapped for beaver. Jim still vividly recalls the misery of the days spent wading through icy water. Although life on the trap lines was hard, Jim found it exciting.

Each spring, when the trapping season was over, Evan came out of the woods, bought Jim a new outfit of "store clothes," and left him with some family to earn his keep doing menial chores. Then Evan would disappear until fall. This was always a hurtful letdown for the sensitive youngster who hated the coming of summer, and was bewildered by Evan's disappearances. Come fall, and trapping time, however, Evan would reappear from nowhere, pick up his boy, and set out for another grueling winter in the woods. The third year, when Jim was twelve years old, Evan failed to show up. Jim never learned what became of him.

At the age of fifteen Jim was expelled from school for smoking cigarettes, and, his education being abruptly ended, he went to sea.

One day while on shore leave in Seattle, he happened to drop into Scott's candy store, where Laurette De Nourde was employed as a clerk. Immediately he became as familiar a fixture as the gumdrop display.

Laurette, like Jim, had been orphaned early in life, but she finished public school in Seattle and then went to work. When her foster parents moved away, she was befriended by the Scotts, who owned a candy store. Laurette helped at the store, learned housekeeping and cooking, and took piano lessons. She had a naturally sweet and clear soprano voice and eventually began singing and playing professionally. That promising career ended at the age of twenty-two, when she met Jim Stanton. Finally, Jim gave up the sea, bought a garage, and, not long after, they were married.

In time, they bought a small, powered rowboat and spent many long, happy week ends fishing and exploring the countryside. They dreamed of the day when Jim might give up his garage and leave them free to explore the wilderness together. Finally the time came when Jim sold his business, pocketed the money, and headed for the north woods. In Vancouver they bought a boat and supplies and embarked on a long fishing trip. They have never come back!

From Queen Charlotte Strait the boat proceeded up the narrower Johnstone Strait and in a few days Jim and Laurette reached the mouth of the Adams River. Here they had to buck their way across a long flat in shallow water. Water shipped in, drenching all their supplies. Once across the flat, they ran in to the beach to dry out, where Jim built a fire; they spread out their wet gear, and Laurette heated dinner from cans. Later they set up the tent and unrolled their sleeping bags.

Suddenly a group of Indians appeared in the little circle of light. Jim and Laurette uneasily studied the impassive faces of their uninvited guests. In an effort to make friends, Laurette picked up a stick that had been chewed by a beaver.

"You catch-um beaver?" she politely inquired, pointing to the tooth marks.

"No catch-um," the tallest Indian replied.

"Catch-um fish?"

"Ugh, plenty salmon catch-um."

"Good Indian," Laurette said approvingly, but the stony-faced redskins did not smile. "Good-by," she added inanely.

The Indians made no reply but disappeared into the darkness as suddenly as they had come.

A week later they stopped at one of the fish cannery stores, which are found along the British Columbia coast line, for the rare luxury of a real meal. As they were purchasing meat and vegetables, a tall, familiar-looking Indian came into the store.

"Good afternoon, Chief," the clerk said deferentially. "Here are some folks who have come up in a rowboat from Vancouver."

"I would be very happy to meet them," the Indian said with a smile, "though it seems to me that we have seen each other before."

13

"Mr. and Mrs. Stanton," the clerk said, "this is Chief Harry Mountain."

"How do you do?" Laurette said blushing.

"The chief," the clerk explained, "is a graduate of the University of British Columbia, and captain of a seine boat in these parts."

"Why didn't you tell me," Laurette demanded, "who you were when we met that night on the beach?"

"You sounded so funny," the chief said, "that I didn't want to destroy the illusion."

Jim stared at Laurette solemnly. "Ugh," he said. "You catch-um fish-um?"

The cannery man told them that the best place for trout was Lake Atluck, so, following his directions, they pushed up the Nimpkish River, a trip that took three days. On the way they went through thirty-six rapids in six miles; Laurette lined the boat from the bank, and Jim, waist-deep in the white, boiling water, guided it clear of the rocks.

At last they were able to make camp and rest on the shore of the wild, lovely little lake. The first morning they awoke to discover that they had had a visitor during the night. Fresh cougar tracks circled their silk tent. Every morning for two weeks they saw new tracks, but not once did they meet the curious cautious cat.

There were no other camps on the lake, but Jim had the distinct feeling that they and the cougar were not its only inhabitants.

"Someone's in here," he told Laurette, "and they don't want to meet us."

Laurette scoffed at the notion, but Jim's ears had not deceived him. Late one night he shook Laurette awake.

"Listen!" he whispered. "Oarlocks. Someone is out on the lake right now."

The next morning Jim found a splash of blood on a log. "I think it's trappers," he said. "I wonder why they're hiding from us?"

That afternoon he made a complete circuit of the lake, gliding swiftly yet soundlessly through the woods, the way he had been taught years before. "You learn to walk in the woods," Jim explained to Laurette, "as you learn to dance. You look ten feet ahead of you and then advance. Your mind records every obstruction before you, and you automatically step over them without making any noise."

Jim found the trappers in their camp hidden deep in the woods—two giant, black-bearded brothers who dwarfed Jim's scant five feet six inches. When they saw that Jim was friendly, they told him their story.

They were Alaskan sourdoughs, nicknamed Baldy and Bones. They had, they said, trapped in Alaska for two years until they had accumulated a big pile of furs. Their gear was packed and they were ready to go when they spotted a grizzly. Getting their guns, they headed after him.

They got their bear, but when they returned to camp they found that it had burned to the ground. A spark from the breakfast fire had evidently blown on their gear. For their two years of hard work they now had nothing but the clothes on their backs and their guns. They had then left Alaska and wandered down into British Columbia. When they found Lake Atluck without a soul on it, they settled down to trap for a season. (There were no registered trap lines then; a man was free to trap anywhere he took a notion to.) When the Stantons appeared on the lake, the sourdoughs naturally assumed that they were trappers who had come to horn in on them.

Jim assured them that he and Laurette weren't trapping, and took the two bearded giants back to his camp to meet Laurette.

"A woman!" they exclaimed in unison.

They had spied on the newcomers; the sourdoughs admitted what Jim already knew. But in her fishing pants and shirt, with a cap pulled down over her hair, they had figured that Laurette was a boy.

They had seen so few women in recent years that they were clumsily unsure of how to act. But when Laurette offered them fresh home made bread, with butter and jam, and hot tea, they relaxed and swapped information with Jim.

"We went up into Knight Inlet," Bones told them. "Heard that's the wildest spot in British Columbia. But it was too wild for us. Too many grizzlies up there."

"Grizzlies!" Jim felt a familiar prickle of hair on the back of his neck.

"Grizzlies!" Laurette echoed. "Knight Inlet, you say? Well, that's where we're going. Right, Jim?"

"Don't know as it's any place for a woman." Baldy said. "Nobody lives on the Inlet regular. A few Indians come up in spring for the oolachan run; some in the fall to trap. But nobody lives there permanent—'cept for the watchman they leave at the cannery at Glendale."

"We don't mind being alone," Laurette said.

"Not so long as there are grizzlies to keep us company," Jim added.

"Company, hell!" Baldy exclaimed. "Them grizzlies ain't fitten company for the devil himself!"

The next day Jim and Laurette started packing their rowboat.

"We've got to make it fast, dear," Jim said. "Up in this

country, winter blows in mighty fast. If we get caught out in it, we're done for."

"It's hard to believe—everything looks so lovely now."

"Don't let it fool you. Besides, our cash has been going out while nothing's been coming in."

"We've still got over eight hundred dollars, Jim."

"It might take all of that just for our winter supplies. Those sourdoughs told me everything is high because it costs so much to transport it up here in the woods."

"Is it that bad, Jim?"

"Let's get going, darling," he said, avoiding her eyes.

They headed down the Nimpkish River for Knight Inlet. Though it had taken them three days to make the run upriver, they whipped down in only two hours. At Johnstone Strait, they confidently headed toward the mouth of the Inlet. Halfway, they hit a cross sea and their heavily laden boat suddenly began to fill.

They finally reached the lee of one of the many islands which clog the strait, and were able to rest for a few minutes. Then they went out again into the wild water and fought their way toward the mouth of the Inlet, where Baldy and Bones had told them they could get fresh supplies.

Minstrel Island, however, was deserted, and the frame hotel building they had seen from the water proved to be empty.

There was nothing, the sourdoughs had informed them, from Minstrel Island to Glendale Cove, a third of the way up the Inlet; then nothing from Glendale to the Head, where there was an Indian camp. Finally, they reached Glendale, where a fish cannery was open and a store which supplied the itinerant fishermen, hand loggers, and Indians who came into the Inlet during the warm months of the year.

By this time it was dusk, so after hastily loading in meat and groceries, they went upstream looking for a place to camp.

The next morning they awoke to a veritable paradise. From their secluded bay they looked out at a magnificent, untouched world. Before them, deep glacial water wound between pine-covered shores for miles. Snow-covered peaks rose twelve thousand feet and more. Natural waterfalls striped the dark forest with silver ribbons. The Inlet water itself was a mysterious opaque green, colored by the flow from the great ice fields above.

They cruised slowly up Knight Inlet toward its head. Virgin timber and unclimbed mountains stretched before them endlessly. Giant pillars of trees rose hundreds of feet into the air. There was a strangely silent, primeval quality to the forest and shores.

Jim pointed across to the western shore, at a point about six miles from Glendale.

"Look over there, dear. Looks like an abandoned cabin. Bet it's a trapper's or logger's place. Probably nobody's lived there for years."

And when they pulled in to the beach, they found that Jim had been right; it was deserted. A solidly built, one-room logger's cabin, it was made of cedar shakes, and the roof was still sound. The interior was a tangled mass of leaves interlaced with mouse trails.

"Well, it's not exactly a palace," Laurette said, "but it would be better than a silk tent in the winter."

"Looks solid enough," Jim said. "And I could fix it up a little—that is, if you want to stay."

It was as simple as that. Making brush brooms, they swept out the cabin and carried in their gear from the boat. Then they took the hour's run down the Inlet to the cannery store for supplies, and told the watchman that they had taken possession of the deserted cabin.

"Old cabin 'bout seven-eight miles from here?" the watchman said. "That's Kwalate."

"Kwa-la-te?" Laurette repeated.

"Indian name," the old fellow explained. "Means 'place of many berries.' You ain't intending to stay there, are you?"

"Why not?" Jim asked.

"Well," the watchman said, shaking his head disapprovingly, "it don't make sense to me, but I s'pose it's your own business." He peered over his glasses at Laurette. "There ain't nothing around there, ma'am, 'cepting wild animals. Some Indians come in the spring and fall, and a few worthless tramps wander around in the summer. Then there's the grizzlies. Lord, man, you don't dare go to the outhouse without a high-powered gun. Just last winter one bear killed a couple of Indians who were trapping up at the Head. And don't ever forget them devils can swim! Why, one of 'em killed an Indian, and then chased his wife down the Klinaklini River with her in a canoe. Followed her for two solid miles whilst she was paddling as hard as she could go. Only just happened some Indians saw her coming and started shooting at the grizzly, or he would have gotten her, too."

"They can be mean," Jim agreed.

"You kidding, fellow? They can be mighty mean. Why, I shoot every grizzly I see! But nothing can get rid of 'em out here. All they do is move back a way into the forest. We got woods and mountains here no man dares go into. The grizzlies are thick up in there."

Jim only smiled.

The cannery man snorted in disgust. "If you ask me, fellow, I think you're plumb crazy!"

2

Window in the Woods

It was early in August, 1919, when Laurette and Jim moved into the Kwalate cabin. As Jim had said, there was no time to waste in preparing for the long winter ahead. They must make their cabin snug and comfortable, estimate their winter's food supplies—keeping in mind their limited budget—and get the order in postehaste, for the last boat of the season came into the mouth of Knight Inlet in early November. From then until April they would—whatever might happen—be strictly on their own. They checked food prices at Glendale and found that, including transportation, they were even higher than had been expected. The provisions for the winter months would take nearly all of the eight hundred dollars that was left.

Jim's frown deepened. He would have to start trapping as soon as the season set in. If his trapping was successful and if fur prices were right, they would have enough money to get through the following summer. Although he had no doubt of his ability as a woodsman, this was strange country, and many things could go wrong. Not wanting to increase Laurette's worries, he kept his thoughts to himself.

Coming back from Glendale, they walked from their boat up toward the cedar-shingled cabin which would be their home for their first winter in the woods.

"Scared?" Jim asked.

"Oh, Jim!" Laurette spread her arms wide in a gesture of delight, as her eyes swept the empty beach, the little cabin framed by the dark, silent forest, and then the wondrous view. "Why should I be scared with all this?"

"Compared to me," he smiled, "you are big city folk. Those trips we made around Seattle were nothing like what we're facing here. You'll soon find that there's danger everywhere— from deep in the forest right to our cabin door. I don't want to frighten you, dear, but the one thing a woodsman—and woodswoman—must learn above all else is constant caution. When you are in the wilds you must, for your own safety, be afraid."

"Well," she admitted, "maybe I am, just a little. But despite its problems, this is paradise!"

"Is that so? Well, honey, even paradise is going to need plenty of fixing up!"

The cedar-shake cabin proved fundamentally sound but rather less than luxurious. It was literally nothing but four walls, a roof, and a decrepit cast-iron stove. They were forced to make several trips to the cannery, bargaining for old lumber and cheap, secondhand carpenter's tools, which they couldn't afford but had to have.

Jim immediately set to work on the bare essentials of simple living: a bed, a table, and chairs. While Laurette papered the unfinished interior with a roll of building paper she had found at the store, Jim built a platform against one wall. On this they spread their sleeping bags. In addition to a rough but adequate table, Jim made two chairs. There wasn't time to make an extra one for company—but they weren't likely to have visitors until spring.

Over the rafters Jim built platforms for the storage of dry

staples: flour, meal, dried beans, rice. Looking around at their confined quarters, Laurette longed for the spaciousness of her Seattle home, but when she glanced out the open door at the glorious landscape, the momentary desire was gone.

A woodshed was added onto the back of the cabin and a wooden outhouse built fifty feet from the house. Reaching it turned out to be an Alpine struggle through the deep snow on dark and cold nights. And it was an even longer haul to carry water by hand from a spring some fifty yards away.

Living on their boat supplies, the Stantons worked long and hard at the job of turning the rough one room into livable winter quarters. However much they accomplished, there was always more to be done. Jim could tell from Laurette's frequent frowns that she wasn't yet satisfied.

"What this place really needs most," he decided as he studied the holes where two small windows had been broken out, "is some really man-sized windows. Those damned things aren't much more than weasel holes."

Laurette looked thoughtfully through the tiny openings which let in brief blasts of the fresh mountain air.

"As long as you have to fix them, anyway," she suggested, "could you throw them together and make one big window. It would give us a full view of the woods and shore. But I know we can't afford it——"

"No, dear, we can't," he said. "But let's get it, anyway. It'll make a nice contrast to that primitive plumbing I threw together back there in the woods."

In the end, they recklessly put through a rush order to Vancouver for springs and mattress, a set of aluminum pots and pans to replace Laurette's meager camping utensils, a new washtub and scrubboard—and a large pane of glass, three feet by ten.

"And I need fruit jars," Laurette said. "Lots of them. The

Indians were right when they named this the 'place of many berries'—it's chock-full of huckleberries and currants. I want to put up loads for winter."

"You'll have to can meat and fish, too," Jim reminded her. "We can't get enough fresh meat to last; and if we depend on what I can shoot, we may go hungry."

"Do you think we'll have enough money left to pay for the supplies?" Laurette asked.

"I hope so," he said doubtfully.

"But if our money is gone, what will we do in the spring?"

Her question gave Jim the opportunity he had been waiting for. "I'm going trapping as soon as the season sets in. It's the only way to make a living up here in the woods once the snow comes."

With the big pane of glass safely set in place, they had a perfect view, which gave added depth to the little room. Below the window they placed the dining table and the two straight chairs. The spring and mattress made a neat bed more yawningly comfortable than their sleeping bags, and a blue woolen blanket converted it into a daytime couch. The aluminum pans shone brightly from pegs which Jim nailed into the wall near the stove. The fruit jars were lined up along the floor back of the stove.

Laurette anxiously counted the days until their provisions would arrive on the last steamer of the season. Among other things, they had ordered flour, corn meal, carrots, potatoes, onions, canned vegetables, canned milk, jam, macaroni, beans—though Jim hated them, Laurette had insisted on adding them to the list—peanuts, rice, sugar, salt, coffee, tea, yeast, bacon, twenty-five pounds of butter, a crate of eggs, a quarter of beef, and cigarette tobacco for "rolling their own."

Also coming were traps for Jim's winter work, snowshoes and skis, and a shotgun for hunting game birds.

The day the boat was due they hurried up to the cannery. It took several trips up and back to transport their precious cargo. And what a bill they had! Carrots, six dollars a bag; butter, a dollar a pound; potatoes, seven dollars a sack. Their order came to over six hundred dollars; almost all the cash they had left in the world!

The day came when they waved good-by to the old cannery watchman. With the first cold winds, he would hole up in his tight little house. The freeze would come soon, he had told them, and it was doubtful they would see each other during the winter months.

By the time they had hauled the last of their supplies up to the woodshed it was already growing dark, so they put off the long job of sorting and stacking until the next day. After supper they sat looking out of their landscape window over the glimmering moon-glossed water.

"See there," Jim nodded, "a beaver moon. We've been doing the same thing as all the animals and woodsfolk and farmers the country over—preparing for winter, tightening our houses, and getting in our supplies."

3

Living Off the Land

"Where will we put all those new supplies?" Laurette asked worriedly. "There's certainly no room in here, and if we leave food out in the shed, it'll freeze and spoil."

"I'm going to dig a cellar," Jim told her. "I'll make a hatch right here in the center of the floor, so we can get to it without going outside. Then I'll dig away enough dirt to make a storeroom. It won't freeze up—the banked snow around the cabin keeps the earth below from freezing. We can store the perishables there, and the food you are going to can."

So far they had been living on fish. The idea of walking out in her own yard and coming back within a quarter hour with a mess of trout or salmon never failed to thrill Laurette. Back in Seattle it had meant miles of driving to reach a good fishing lake; and often they came back without a catch. But here, scarcely more than a stone's throw from their door, was the point where the Kwalate River flowed into Knight Inlet and where coho, sockeye, and dog salmon could be had at will. There were steelheads, too, the delicious rainbow trout which had come up from the sea. They showed more fight than the coho, and it sometimes took a half-hour to land one.

Crowding back of the cabin, clustering the woods around,

almost down to the waterline of the beach, were berries in profusion. The velvety red salmonberries were almost gone now, but silver currants and huckleberries, which ranged from blue to red and jet black, were still abundant. Interspersed among the berry brambles were small, gnarled wild crab apple trees from which the diminutive fruit hung in clusters. Laurette worked feverishly to pick the fruit and preserve it before the season would pass. The apples she canned in a heavy syrup, keeping them on their stems in the original clusters. When they first dined on wild duck—so plentiful that Jim said he could have shot one with his eyes closed— she opened a jar of the crab apples, and their tartness combined with the gamey taste of the duck proved to be a culinary sensation.

It was fortunate that there were ducks for the taking, that Laurette's canned fish didn't spoil, and that the deer Jim shot found its way into corned venison packed into fruit jars, for the supplies they had purchased turned out to be almost entirely worthless.

Jim had brought in the sacks from the woodshed and Laurette opened them.

"Just look, Jim," she cried, "these carrots are almost rotten!"

"And they cost six dollars a bag." Jim anxiously examined them through the netting and saw the rotting ends. Tossing the bag aside, he lifted the sack of potatoes and hefted it, puzzled. "Didn't we order fifty pounds of spuds?"

"Fifty? I thought it was a hundred."

"Well, this isn't over twenty-five." Jim lit a cigarette and puffed on it rapidly. "We can't spare the money to buy more— and it's too late to get them, anyway."

"We have plenty of macaroni and beans, thank heaven," Laurette sighed. "We'll have to make do with them."

"You can have the beans," Jim said.

The dry supplies went up on the rafter boards, the few potatoes and the spoiled carrots were stored in the cellar, and then Laurette prepared the other supplies for storing. She dipped the bacon into melted paraffin as a seal. Then came the eggs. Laurette had ordered waterglass, the traditional fluid compound used for preserving eggs. She made up the solution, put the eggs in crocks, and they were lowered into the cellar.

The butter was next. Laurette believed it should be salted, and eyed the twenty-five pounds unhappily. It turned out, as she had surmised, to be a laborious job. She worked elbow-deep in the yellow mass, forcing additional salt into it with her fingers.

By fishing daily, they caught enough to can. Jim cleaned them, and Laurette cut them into serving-sized pieces and soaked them for an hour in brine. Then she drained and packed them, with no additional liquid, into glass jars, which she boiled for four hours in the washtub. After sealing and wrapping the jars, she later stored them in the cellar. The quarter of beef she corned before canning, too.

They were able to get only two meals from the whole six-dollar bag of carrots. The corn meal was laced with weevils. The pile of potatoes dwindled rapidly, and within a month, to Jim's disgust, macaroni and beans were constantly on the menu. Even the canned vegetables were so old the contents had actually rusted the interior of the cans. After scraping out what she could salvage from the mess, Laurette boiled the vegetables thoroughly before serving them in the hope of killing whatever deadly germs they might contain.

Their first taste of the heavily salted butter nearly choked them. From then on, Laurette took some butter out hours ahead of a meal, and washed it over and over, removing as much salt as she could.

"I am sure," she announced after several weeks, "that there is a much better way of keeping butter. And eggs, too. I simply can't stand the taste of these except in hotcakes or cake."

"Well, you figure it, honey," Jim teased. "Nobody else has managed to in all the years people have lived in the woods. But I wouldn't be at all surprised if you do."

"Don't think I can't," Laurette said briskly. "By next winter I'll have it all figured out."

"That," Jim quietly reminded her, "depends on whether we're still here, then."

"Don't you think we will be?"

"Well, we're just about broke," he said. "And the only way to make any money before spring is by trapping. I haven't trapped since I was a kid. And besides, I don't know these woods—they're a damned sight wilder than anything I've ever been in before."

"And if it doesn't work out?"

"We'll have to go back to Seattle."

"Oh, Jim, no!"

That night Laurette lay quietly beside Jim in the bed but her eyes were wide open until dawn.

As the chill fall days closed in on them, Jim went out to inspect the nearby forest. There was no longer a market for the black bear he and Evan Evenson had trapped long ago. As for grizzlies, Jim had no thought of hunting them and selling the hides. Later on he had an idea he might guide big-game hunters to them. But he couldn't conceive of shooting the majestic beasts himself.

In the great forest that stretched back of their cabin up

toward the high peaks above them, and along the banks of the Kwalate River, was evidence of mink, otter, and marten. Choking undergrowth covered much of the woods, and in many areas there was a floor of fallen trees; these had piled up and rotted upon one another since time began, making passage well-nigh impossible. Before he began trapping, he had to make certain that there was a cleared trail to follow and a well-stocked cabin he could get to in case of emergency. Jim would have to be alone on the trap line—for Laurette would certainly not be able to bear the sight of a captured animal struggling for its life.

He must plan with the utmost care. In trapping alone in the forest the greatest danger lay in the possibility of breaking a leg and, unable to walk, freezing to death in the open. He decided to lay out fifteen miles of trap line, beginning at their house, and leading five miles back into the woods to a small natural clearing of level ground, which would be suitable for an overnight cabin. From there he planned to clear out a loop line to the junction of two forks of the river. This would place his farthest trap within easy reach of shelter.

He blazed his trap line and then set out with Laurette to clear the trail. The underbrush was so thick that it took them all day, working from daybreak to dark, to cut away a path which could then be traversed within minutes. As they progressed farther from the house, they carried provisions and sleeping equipment so they wouldn't lose time going back and forth.

Laurette's hundred pounds were distributed in hard muscles over her five feet four inches. It was no trick for her to swing an ax or machete, or to carry her twenty-five-pound pack for many miles. Two inches taller and fifty pounds heavier, Jim carried twice as heavy a pack strapped over his shoulders.

At night they made camp wherever they were and cooked

over an open fire. Finally, they reached the spot which Jim had selected for his cabin. In a short time they felled small trees and built a tiny, rough cabin of logs. "So small," Jim observed, "that I can sit in bed and cook my supper." Since a trapper uses his cabin only after dark, coming in at night and leaving before daylight, they did not bother with windows, and the door was the only opening.

They went back home and soon after Jim prepared to set out alone, with his traps and bait.

"I don't like leaving you down here by yourself," he said. "But there's no way out of it."

"I couldn't stand seeing those poor animals being killed," she needlessly reminded him.

"It's their life or ours," he pointed out. "With marten averaging thirty-three dollars a skin, and mink eight dollars, I may be able to clear enough this season to pay for next winter's groceries."

"Yes, I know. And I won't really be alone, Jim. There's always something around—birds, squirrels, deer. Why, just this morning a mama porcupine came to the door."

As Jim dogtrotted down the rough path, he reflected that they had done everything possible to anticipate emergencies. The cabin was stocked with a two-week supply of firewood, and staple foods were stored in a cache under the cabin floor. In case he might be unable to make the cabin or their house by nightfall, Jim carried a sleeping bag and silk fly in his pack. His clothes followed the trapper's maxim: "Wear all the clothes you own, and then put something windproof over all of it." He wore two sets of cotton underwear—cotton dries faster than wool and it is usually very wet deep in the forest—and two pairs of heavy socks. Over this were a thick wool shirt, rubber pants, and logger's calked boots with nine-inch tops and half-inch spikes of tempered steel. An over-sized heavy rubber coat hung from his shoulders, covering both his pack and himself. In his pockets he carried a com-pass, staples to fasten the traps, flashlight, matchbox and tobacco can, both waterproof, pocket knife, whetstone, am-munition—and peanuts and candy to munch as he trotted along the trail in the tireless dogtrot which he had learned from Evan, and which he is still able to maintain all day. He also carried his 30.30 rifle and a machete—a long, curved knife with which he chopped branches and small brush from his path.

Jim worked his way along, setting traps. His quarry were the aristocrats of the weasel family: mink and marten. All marten will take bait. But along the beach, where part of his line ran, only a sick mink will go for bait since there is plenty of natural food available. The only way to capture the wily fellows was to get them when they were moving at top speed. So Jim used trail sets for the mink, placing un-baited traps lengthwise on the open trail. He dug little holes into the earth to conceal the traps, then led the trap chain to a springy bush and fastened it; in that way the animal would be unable to get a solid hold and pull free. He used Number O jump traps, which neither kill nor permanently injure the animal. If he caught a female, he intended to turn her loose so she could go on breeding.

As he worked, Jim studied the silent forest around him with keen interest. This was much wilder country than that he had traveled with Evan. This was grizzly country, and he thought of the tales he had heard from trappers, Indians, and garrulous old woodsmen of hand-to-hand combats between man and the Lord of the Woods. Now that he was in the north country, he was eager to meet his first grizzly face to face.

When he reached the fork of the river, he took out his fishing tackle to catch some trout for his midday meal. He walked down the bank, then suddenly stopped and stared. There in the wet sand were fresh tracks, the sides sharp and newly made. They were ten-inch tracks, with well-defined claw marks in front, tapering sharply at the heel. They were pushed deep into the sand with the weight of five hundred pounds or more.

A grizzly!

Quietly Jim padded down the bank, following the tracks. Suddenly the sound of crackling brush reached his ear. Silently lowering himself to the ground, he inched forward toward a big windfallen tree a few yards into the forest. The bear was up on that tree, tearing at berry bushes with his big paws. Jim eased along the length of the tree until he could see the animal. But it wasn't a grizzly; it was just a big black bear. Grizzlies, Jim was learning, were wary creatures who kept out of sight until they "got used to you."

Jim lifted his rifle and fired into the shadowy head, then quickly jumped back under the tree so that the animal wouldn't roll on him. There was a soft groan, a slump, and the crashing of a heavy body across the log. He waited a few seconds longer, for safety's sake, until assured by the silence that the bear was dead. Then he cautiously got up and stepped on top of the log.

He stripped the black bear's hide to make a rug for his trap-line cabin. He also cut off some tenderloin for steaks; though grizzly meat is usually rank and fishy, the flesh of a black bear can be fairly good eating. Then he went back to the tracks he had followed. They were grizzly tracks, all right; he was positive of that. But what had happened to the animal?

How could so huge a beast disappear so completely and mysteriously?

He spent that night in his cabin but before daylight the next morning he had started to set his traps on his loop line, eight miles inland from the beach. The first fall of snow had dropped a thick white covering over the woods, and it was lonely working by himself. When he was a day away from his trapping cabin and two days from home, he almost wished that he had let well enough alone and stopped at the five-mile cabin instead of going so far into the forest.

And then he heard a sudden cry. Not that of a bird or any animal he recognized, but horrible, chilling, human laughter. The raucous joy of a madman, blood-curdling and hideous. He automatically stepped from the trail, hid behind a tree, and listened. Again it came, ripping the curtains of silence—high, cackling, witless, hanging eerily in the air.

He had heard tales of men lost in the lonesome forest who, driven by fear and desperation, had become hopelessly insane. His hand slid back along the barrel of his gun and slipped the safety catch. But, he thought while his index finger rested lightly on the trigger, you can't shoot down a man in cold blood. Not even if he has gone mad.

The laugh came again, shrill, mindless. This time he located it in a patch of evergreen less than a hundred yards away. It wasn't courage that drove him into the forest. In the forest, caution is more valuable than courage. It was the thought that with a madman wandering the woods, Laurette, alone in their home, would be in constant danger.

Gripping his rifle firmly, Jim quietly moved ahead. When he finally reached the evergreen, he softly parted the clump of dense bush. At first he saw nothing. Then, dropping his eyes, he stared in surprise, not at a raving human, but at a sullen male porcupine!

The old male lifted its head and laughed again—that wild, eerie cry which was his mating call. Then Jim broke into laughter. He laughed so hard that tears rolled down his leathered cheeks. And the startled porcupine, hearing the strange bellowing of this obviously insane creature, turned and darted off into the woods.

4

Merry Christmas!

When Jim returned to the cabin a couple of days later, Laurette faced him with a problem.

"The yeast's almost gone," she said. "I'm down to my last cake—and this is only December!"

Jim shook his head and went out to the woodpile, where he chopped away as he mulled over this new problem, leaving Laurette slumped mournfully over her one yeast cake.

Suddenly he came dashing back to the house. "I've got it!" he cried. "If you have that one cake, can't you make some kind of starter with it—a flour and water paste that keeps working, as they do for sourdough?"

"That's an idea!" Laurette's face brightened. "I remember when I was a little girl I used to see Mother make her own yeast cakes when her supply ran out." She deliberated a moment. "Seems to me she used corn meal rather than flour——"

After supper, while Laurette sifted her weevily corn meal and mixed it with water to make a thick paste, Jim cut a piece of wire screen and stretched it out on the shelves above the stove. Laurette added her one yeast cake to the corn meal paste, then spread the mixture on the wire screen, where it was left to dry out. "Would Jim's idea work?" she wondered anxiously.

Next day, when the dough was thoroughly dried and brittle, she cut it into squares and used one to make a batch of bread. She watched happily as the dough rose perfectly, just as it had with the storemade yeast.

"Didn't I tell you?" Laurette exulted as she stored the rest of the cakes away in a tin. "There's always a way—if you just take time to figure it out!"

When the severe winter blizzards came, the snow banked up around the house and, as Jim had predicted, insulated it against the winter cold so that the food stored beneath the floor did not freeze. The old iron stove kept the cabin cozy —so warm, in fact, that when Laurette was baking and keeping the fire high, they often opened the door to get fresh air.

Before they knew it, it was December. Their first Christmas in the north woods was a simple one. Jim cut down a small spruce, and Laurette decorated it with stars and wreaths cut out of old wrapping paper; she hung them from pieces of string which she had dipped in a jar of preserved berries to give them color. There was neither tinsel nor candles, but when she had finished decorating the tree, her eyes shone.

A day before Christmas, Jim went out on his trap line to see what he had caught. Since trapping was their only hope of having any money in the spring, he didn't dare waste a day.

Jogging along the trail, he wondered what he could give Laurette. There was no money to spare; and since they were snowed in for the winter, no place to buy anything. In Seattle they had always had a Christmas tree; they would have one today, too, but this year there wouldn't be any gifts around it.

In the last trap on the trail Jim found a young female porcupine. She looked up at him pathetically, silently begging to be freed, and Jim was about to let her go when he suddenly remembered—the porky would be his Christmas gift to

Laurette! Putting the animal in a bag, he started for home. As he neared the cabin early Christmas morning, Jim took out the porcupine, held it up, and shouted:

"Merry Christmas!"

Laurette flung open the door and stared with surprise and pleasure at the squirming porcupine, the strangest Christmas gift she had ever received.

"Happy holiday, dear," Jim said.

Laurette curtsied formally. "And a very merry Christmas to you, darling!"

When Jim set the porcupine down, she ran to a corner of the room and stood there with her head to the wall. Laurette went to her supply shelf and, getting a handful of dried prunes, put them on the floor where the shy animal could smell them. Her nose finally getting the best of her, she turned around and ate the prunes.

"That porcupine," Laurette said happily, "is the nicest Christmas present I ever had. And for you, Jim, I've baked a cake!"

Before they ate, she poured berry juice and they silently drank a toast in celebration of their first Christmas in the north woods. After supper, they rolled cigarettes and smoked them lazily while sipping their coffee.

"Are you happy, dear?" Jim asked.

"Gloriously!"

Late that night the porcupine became restless, and Laurette let her out the door, but early next morning they heard a scratch. When Laurette opened the door, Lady Porcupine bounced into the cabin, acting very pleased and excited. From that time on, until she went into the seclusion of the woods in March to bear her young, the porcupine was a daily caller.

When mice began raiding their meager supplies, Jim caught

a weasel in a box trap and brought it in to rid the cabin of the pests. The bold, savage little beast soon did the job and eventually became so tame he took meat from Laurette's fingers without biting her. This was a real victory since, of all the weasel family, King Ermine is the most savage and least tractable. But, as an old trapper later remarked to Jim, "That woman of yours could tame wildcats!"

Gradually they came to know, and enjoy, all the animals around them. Jim couldn't resist occasionally taking a few minutes off from his trapping to watch the otters at play. Along the beach he often came upon their slides going down from steep bluffs to the water. They would run up to them and then coast belly-down, hitting the water with a great splash. He told Laurette about their antics, and also about the rock rabbits who, resembling small Belgian hares, are great husbandmen.

"They are the damnedest little things," he said chuckling. "They run all over cutting hay, and lay it out in the sun to cure before storing it for the winter. If it rains, they race around and pull it inside their rock burrows. They act just like the farmers I worked for when I was a kid."

Long before winter was over they used the last of the canned corned meat and fish from their basement store.

"I'll just have to get some fresh meat," Jim said. "I wish you'd go with me on a hunting trip."

"Can't we just make it a camping trip," she pleaded, "and let the hunting go until another day?"

"And in the meantime eat beans? No thank you!"

It was a beautiful crisp winter day with no wind blowing when, with loaded packs on their backs, they headed up the trail toward the mountains. High up in the timber, as they moved out into a clearing, they came upon a family of white mountain goats which looked up curiously, sniffing and staring at the strangers, but making no move to run off.

Jim, whose rifle was ready in his hand, lowered the barrel uncertainly. "I suppose they never saw humans before," he said.

Laurette turned to her husband. "You can't shoot anything that just stands and looks at you, can you, Jim?"

He put down his rifle with a sigh. "No, dear," he quietly agreed. "Not even for a month's supply of fresh meat!"

After dining disconsolately on beans, they spent the night at the trapping cabin, and then headed back home.

The winds howled and snow fell endlessly until it nearly reached the eaves of their cabin. They lost track of the days and dates; time seemed to stand still.

Keeping up a supply of firewood was in itself a full-time job. Then there was the eternal round of hauling water, feeding the animals that crept timidly near the door when deep snow covered their feeding grounds, keeping the fire going in their old iron stove, and trying every possible variation on the monotonous theme of macaroni, beans, and dried peas. Each night found them piling gratefully into the platform bed and falling into the deep sleep of the physically exhausted.

But as Laurette's stock of canned goods diminished, Jim's pile of furs grew. Each round on his trap line produced valuable pelts of marten and mink. They would bring the money urgently needed for next winter's food—if all went well.

At last the backbone of winter was broken, and spring was upon them. The mountains began to resume the deep shadows of summer, the water regained its green brilliance, and when they opened their cabin door in the morning, a fresh warm sun blessed their faces.

The third week in April, when the ice had cleared away

so that boats could run the Inlet again, they had their first callers: two Royal Canadian Mounted Police. The Mounties looked around the snug cabin in amazement.

"We heard there was a couple trying to get through the winter up here," they said. "But we never expected to find them alive!"

Laurette fed the husky, hungry men what her slim larder could provide, padding the meal with plenty of warm, home-made bread, hot coffee, and the last of her currant jam. They ate gratefully, drinking cup after cup of the scalding coffee. Finally they were on their way, waving good-by as their little gas-boat sped up the Inlet.

"How does it feel," Jim asked, "to see other human beings again?"

"You know," Laurette replied, "we've been so darn busy, I haven't even had time to miss them!"

Since most bears hibernate through the deep winter, it was not until spring that Jim met his first grizzly. He was walking along the beach with Laurette. The water was lazy and green; the forests were dropping their dark shrouds; animals came out of the woods and hustled along on their eternal search for food.

"Sh-h-h!" Jim suddenly stopped. "There's something big back there in the forest."

"Let's go see."

"Follow me." Jim gripped his gun and stepped silently into the trees, his free hand guiding Laurette. Soon his keen eyes discerned the shadow of a large, lumbering creature, and he drew Laurette behind the protection of a windfall log.

As they watched, a sow grizzly came out into a little clearing. She moved slowly and deliberately, seemingly without purpose until, a few moments later, a big boar appeared, sniffing her tracks. She made no attempt to get away and he soon caught up with her.

He backed off and, with startling suddenness, lifted an immense paw and belted her across the shoulders and head. The blow was so swift and strong that it sent her tumbling end over end. Getting to her feet with a purposeful look, she crossed to the boar and smacked him back. But he stood his ground, reached out his paw and struck her again, sending her rolling to the ground once more.

The sow got up, looked at him and, as if acknowledging that he was master of the situation, dutifully squatted. The boar immediately mounted her and finished his business in short order. Then he climbed down and nonchalantly strolled off into the woods, and she wandered away in another direction. The whole matter had been consummated in less than five minutes.

Jim watched slyly as the color rose up Laurette's throat and suffused her cheeks. He broke out laughing, and then said something which Laurette remembers to this day.

"Civilization," he commented reflectively, "tries to hide what Nature unashamedly accepts."

5

Empty Pockets

The first steamer from Vancouver finally arrived at Glendale, and Jim shipped his furs to the city. At the same time he placed a rush order for desperately needed provisions. While he was at the cannery, making these arrangements, he noticed two old sailboat hulls lying alongside the steamer.

"One of those might make us a good gas-boat," he said to Laurette.

"If you could get it at a bargain, and the engine didn't cost too much."

"It would be handy for long trips and for hauling supplies."

Jim studied the boats. They appeared to be identical: Columbia River boats, 27 feet long with 7-foot 6-inch beams and a depth of 2½ feet. On closer inspection, however, only one hull proved to be sound. Jim knew enough about ship carpentry to build a cabin, a skeg, and install an engine which would convert the hull into the sort of boat they wanted. But since the furs hadn't yet been sold, they had only a hundred dollars left over after buying the previous winter's supplies, and that would be needed for the engine and other things to convert the hull into a good boat. If he went ahead with the deal, they would be practically penniless. He'd have to bargain sharply.

When he asked about them, the cannery man shrugged. "You can have them both for fifty dollars."

"I only want one," Jim said casually. "Neither is in very good shape."

"Not much more'n junk," the seller agreed.

"How about that one?" Jim pointed to the unsound hull.

"You can have it for twenty-five."

Jim pretended to ponder for a moment. "I think the other one would do me." He pointed to the sound hull. "Looks pretty worn, but I could give you, say, fifteen dollars for it, and patch it up myself."

"Take it," the man said.

A few weeks later the second callers of the season arrived, an attractive pair of bachelors: an Englishman, Tommy Bartlett, and his Swedish partner, Martin Peterson. They were hand loggers who came regularly to the Inlet each spring to hand-log enough of the giant timber to support themselves through the following year. They arrived in a gas-boat, towing behind it a well-furnished house-float run by their motherly housekeeper, Mrs. Forest, who cooked and cared for them—and raised cats on the side. Laurette was immediately enchanted with Mrs. Forest's pets, and soon became the owner of three toms.

Jim, meanwhile, listened with interest to the loggers as they explained how they worked. The money for his furs hadn't arrived yet, and the old hull and the equipment he had ordered for it had taken every last cent.

"Why don't you join us?" Bartlett said. "We'll split three ways."

"But I've never hand-logged in my life. I wouldn't be able to earn my share."

"You'd learn fast," Peterson promised. "Any man who can

trap in here alone all winter must be a good woodsman. It wouldn't take you any time to get the hang of it."

Jim wasn't so sure. However, a few days later, when the freighter came back, his decision was made for him. The postwar slump of World War I had hit the fur market. Jim's beautiful marten skins, which had averaged $33 each when Jim began trapping, brought only $4 a skin, and his prime mink sold for $1.50 each instead of the $8 of the previous fall. His total earnings for the trapping season came to around two hundred dollars!

"I didn't want you to go trapping!" Laurette cried.

"Now, darling," he said soothingly, taking her into his arms, "try to look on the bright side."

"But there isn't any," she sobbed. "And even if there was, we couldn't stay on. We'll have to go back to Seattle!"

"Maybe," Jim said, trying to sound cheerful, "I can team up with those loggers. They've already asked me."

"But you don't know the first thing about hand logging."

"I'll learn," he said grimly. "I've got to!"

Most of the men who made their living in the woods in those days stuck to one trade: they were either hand loggers, trappers, or fishermen. But, although there was a spring season on several fur-bearing animals, Jim did not want to trap in the spring. By leaving them alone during their breeding season, trapping only in fall and winter, and turning females loose where possible, he would eventually be asssured of a good supply of animals.

"We'll leave our housekeeper here to keep Mrs. Stanton company," Bartlett said.

Laurette's summer promised to be a busy one. Mrs. Forest suggested that they can together and divide what they put up. She had devised a perfect way to can fresh meat and, in addition to fruit, they would order a side of beef to put up while the men were away logging. Mrs. Forest did not corn or pickle the meat, as Laurette had; she cut the raw meat into bite-sized chunks, put it into glass jars with a teaspoonful of salt, and no liquid. Then she boiled the jars. The beef, or venison, drawn by the salt, formed its own rich juice, which could be used in stews, gravies, or casserole dishes. Her method also worked in canning fish. Unfortunately, however, Mrs. Forest didn't have any new suggestions to offer for keeping butter and eggs.

Jim watched in amazement while his new partners cast appraising glances over apparently similar trees and knew instantly which were worth taking. Of the some five thousand loggers who worked along the coast of British Columbia, he had been lucky enough to tie in with two of the best.

"They don't write insurance for hand loggers," Tommy Bartlett warned him as the gas-boat moved along the Inlet. "It's too easy to get killed. But remember this: most accidents come from being tired. Figure your working day by how you feel rather than by the number of hours you put in. A good logger can make fifty dollars a day. But it won't do him any good if he's dead."

Hand-falling the great cedars, from three to six feet in diameter, is highly skilled as well as dangerous work. Two fallers work together from springboards on opposite sides of the tree, about five feet above the ground. After chopping an undercut on the side they wish the tree to fall, they saw across the back with a six-foot crosscut saw. If the undercut is placed wrong, the tree, when partly sawed, may kick back and kill one of the fallers. If they are working on a steep bluff, the man who is on the bluff side must stay on his springboard when the tree goes over or he will fall.

Jim's first job was to limb the trees the partners had cut while they went on to the next one. When several were felled, limbed, and ready to go, the three men worked together, hoisting the trees with 68-pound Gilchrist jacks, which they had packed up from the boat, and starting them down the slope to the beach. Jacked-up trees might move several hundred yards before they were stopped by windfalls or heavy brush, or, with bad luck, they might get stuck every few feet. Rejacking and chopping away windfalls and brush in the tree's path was back-breaking work.

But once a roadway was cleared from the patch of forest where they were working down to the "chuck," as they called the salt water, the trees roared down faster than they could be handled by the man on the beach. When a number were on their way, the partners stayed with the jacks while Jim went down to the boat to take the trees in tow as they hit the water and herd them into a bag-boom—seven or eight boom sticks connected with chains and floating on the water to form a "pen" for the trees. When several trees had been towed over to the boom, the men joined Jim and with stiff crosscut bucking saws, they sawed the full-length trees into logs. Then the saw logs were racked into sections, and were ready for sale.

One day while Jim was working with the men on the boom out over the water, a forestry boat appeared down the inlet and drew abreast of the boom. Passers-by were sufficiently rare so that all strange boats were a subject for conjecture, interest, and a few minutes off the job. Trying to get a clearer view of the men in the boat, Jim took a step forward; the logs he stood on suddenly parted, and he slipped between them down under the boom. As he came up spluttering, the logs closed over him, pushed in together by the 66-foot-long boom sticks. Though he could push up above water enough to get a breath, there was no opening between the logs for him to pull himself through. The strong current drove against him, so that he could not work his way out the nearest side. Taking a big breath, Jim started swimming. He had no choice but to move with the current down the length of two full sections of logs— over a hundred feet. When he finally emerged at the end of the boom, Bartlett and Peterson, were scampering over the boom, peering around for him anxiously.

"Here I am!" Jim panted, pulling himself over the side.

They ran to him and lifted him to his feet, feeling his body and legs to make certain that he wasn't injured.

"Man alive!" Martin Peterson exclaimed. "What in hell happened to you?"

"First thing we knew," Tommy said, "you had dropped clean out of sight! You must have damned near drowned!"

"Fact of the matter is," Jim quietly admitted, "I very nearly did." Then he told them what had happened.

"It's the first time," Martin said, "that I ever heard of a man's going swimming under a boom—and coming out alive."

"Adds up to what I've said all along," Tommy said thoughtfully. "You've got to have eyes all over your head when you're hand logging."

Jim did what jobs they gave him; meanwhile he watched Martin and Tommy closely, and after they quit work for the day, practised putting in the undercut.

"You're doing fine," Martin said one night as he followed Jim to the tree he was working on. "I don't know whether you know, but Tommy's got a bad heart. If you feel you can work on the springboard, I wish you'd take his place. He might have an attack and fall off that thing. He'll be better limbing 'em up, where he can stop work any time he feels faint."

"All right," Jim agreed hesitantly. He moistened his lips as he felt a sudden dry tension of nervousness. "If you think I can do my part, I'll try."

The following day Jim told Tommy he would like to work the springboard, and Tommy relinquished his spot without question. "Just be careful," he warned.

Both men watched closely while Jim chopped the springboard hole, placed his board, then climbed up on it. Five feet wasn't much, Jim thought, but as he looked from his precarious perch down to the ground that fell away in a steep, rocky incline below him, he realized his danger. If he wasn't balanced just right, if his board wasn't placed just right, he stood a good chance of breaking his neck.

Jim resolutely faced the huge tree trunk and started chopping. Hours later, when the great tree fell, plunging from its tremendous height, Jim felt such a thrill of exhilaration that his whole body trembled. The undercut was right; it was sawed right; the tree fell right—and he had done it.

While Tommy began limbing, Jim and Martin attacked a new tree. Up on his springboard Jim dug his toes in, felt the ease of his muscles settling into place, lifted his ax. Then, looking up, he saw a branch, evidently shaken loose somewhere high in the tree, drifting down directly toward him, and involuntarily he reached out his hand to catch it.

"Pull your arm in and crouch!" Martin yelled.

Jim quickly did as he was told just before the branch, looking much bigger now as it came parallel with his eyes, struck the end of the springboard, tore off a corner, and crashed to earth below him. Then he let go of the trunk he was grasping and stood up uncertainly.

"Don't ever do that again!" Martin shouted. "That's a widow-maker! Way up there it looks small and light—so you reach out, and it either breaks your arm or pulls you off the board. Those branches look harmless up high like that, but they pack power. And don't you forget it."

By the end of the summer the three men had put in three sections of timber—150,000 feet. Two months before, cedar was bringing $44 a thousand feet. When they sold their three sections, the market had dropped to $7.50 a thousand. Jim's earnings for the summer's work were a little over three hundred dollars.

"I guess we're snake bit," he said to Laurette. "When I trap, the market drops; when I log, the market drops. If I become a commercial fisherman, I bet that market will drop, too."

"Well, I know one place the market hasn't fallen," she said. "The cannery store. Potatoes six-fifty a sack! Sugar twenty-five cents a pound! With all the canning I've been doing, that really adds up!"

"How about going back to Seattle? Wages are higher, prices are lower."

"And you," Laurette added, "are out of your mind!"

"We could still get away from here," Jim persisted. "It's summer yet. We could run to Seattle, or into Vancouver, before fall comes."

"If you go back to town," Laurette warned, "you go alone!"

"Three hundred dollars," Jim began figuring. "That with the two hundred from the trap line leaves us only a hundred short of what we paid for food last year."

"We have no rent. And we don't have to buy fish."

"Or deer," he said. "We're allowed two a season."

"Well——Go a long way from the house when you hunt, will you, Jim? I fed a couple last winter, and I couldn't bear it if you killed one of them."

"Before I shoot, I'll ask the deer if he's a friend of yours."

Laurette thanked him with a smile. "I made a garden while you were logging," she said. "We'll have some of our own vegetables this time. I've canned the early berries, fish, and that quarter of beef we bought when the first freighter came in. Another thing," she added with pride, "I think I've figured out a way to do the butter and the eggs, Jim. At least, we'll give it a try."

"I'd sure hate to see you mess up fifty pounds of butter and six crates of eggs!"

"I won't," she promised. "I have a hunch."

Laurette's hunch was based on intuition and a prayer. Why couldn't salt be used without actually penetrating the food? She made a barrel of brine and packed the butter in it, pound by pound, weighting each layer with wooden cask rounds. Then she covered the top with a wooden cover, weighted it with rocks, and left it out in the cool woodshed.

The eggs were more complicated. She bored holes in the bottom of wooden candy buckets, and lined them with dairy salt. Then she melted a kettle of lard, hand-dipped each egg in the lard to seal it, and laid it on the salt bed, small end down, with the air space of the egg on top. When one layer was full, she covered it with salt, then started another, making sure that none of the eggs touched. When the buckets were filled, she covered the top completely with salt, and stacked them in the shed for the winter. As eggs were needed, she washed them in warm water to melt off the coating of lard and salt. Months later, she was able to poach or boil eggs preserved in this manner! Once, for an experiment, she kept some of her eggs fourteen months before using them, and was delighted to find them fresh-tasting as ever.

"You see," she reminded Jim when they finished their first

dozen 'stored' eggs that fall, "it's just a matter of staying in the woods long enough to figure things out!"

By now Laurette and Jim were "old settlers." While their cash had again all gone into foodstuffs, they had found a more reliable outfitter whose staples, though outrageously high when shipped in by freighter, were good quality. A buck deer—no friend of Laurette's—helped stretch out the rows of canned goods; and the meat, fish, vegetables and berries which Laurette had canned during the summer seemed ample to last through a long winter.

The gas-boat was painted and in good working order, for Jim had worked on it during the summer whenever he got back to Kwalate from the logging job. He had installed the engine, put in bunks and a stove, and Laurette had painted it. Then too they had company for the long winter months ahead. Not only were there the three cats, acquired from Mrs. Forest, but there was Bob, a carelessly bred mutt that Jim had picked up at the cannery. Bob's idea of being a good woods dog was to bark at the deer, chase porcupine, and lie as close to the stove as possible.

Again Laurette went out with Jim to help pack supplies into the little cabin and clear the trail for winter trapping. The nights were chilly, and the cry of timber wolves was frightening, but a bright campfire kept them warm and held off the wolves.

Jim had high hopes for his trapping this year. During the summer an old Finn trapper, named Lytie, had stopped by for a visit. He was a tough, old-fashioned trapper, who had no qualms about conservation. He literally cleaned out the country wherever he trapped, stripping it of every fur-bearing animal he found. Using a grizzly hide for a sled to carry his furs, he trapped all over the Arctic, and every spring he came out with a mountain of furs.

Lytie admitted to a strange secret: he had lived with an Indian tribe in the Great Slave country, at the northern limit of timber, and they had given him a tribal secret—a recipe for a scent that would call animals. Perhaps because he was getting too old to trap any longer, or because he just liked Jim, Lytie gave him the secret recipe, and as soon as he had gone on his way, Jim started collecting the ingredients.

They were vile enough to shame Macbeth's trio of witches: rotten meat, rotten liver, rotten fish, asafetida, anise seed oil— and the "mystery ingredient" with the special lure: a pounded weed seed, the name of which Jim has never divulged. It is this which gives the concoction its sex appeal. Jim mixed the ingredients carefully, put the mess in a four-pound jam tin, and set it up on the rafter over the stove to ripen.

However, there was one thing he forgot to do: pound an air hole in the can! Fortunately neither Jim nor Laurette was in the house when the can exploded and the odorous mess flew all over the ceiling, walls, stove, and floor.

Over thirty years later Laurette still recalls the awful smell with a shudder. "I had to scrub every inch of the cabin with Lysol before we could even sleep inside. Believe me, a skunk's charge would be perfume compared to that horrible stuff!"

With typical persistence and curiosity, Jim made a new batch. That fall he carried a small tin of the scent with him and smeared a little dab on trees above his baited marten traps. At first the squirrels were drawn by the scent and got in the sets. After throwing them out for several rounds, Jim set his traps harder; but they were then set too hard for the little martens, who were able to take the bait without springing the traps.

"The trouble with that stuff," Jim complained, "was that it called *all* the animals!"

For Christmas that year Jim brought in a wild goose for dinner; Laurette decorated the cabin with fir and cedar boughs, and then, to Jim's surprise, presented him with a cumbersome box which she had managed to keep hidden since the last freighter.

Jim eagerly opened the box. In it were several sure-kill traps designed to kill instantly the animal that got into them.

"That's so they won't suffer," Laurette explained.

"But they don't suffer in my traps," Jim protested. "My traps don't hurt me—or the animals. When the wrong animal gets in, I can turn it loose, alive and unhurt."

"But you have to kill the right ones!"

"Yes, I do," he admitted. "But these"—he lifted one of the heavy iron traps—"these are man-killers, Laurette. If I ever caught a finger or hand in one of these things, I'd be sunk."

"But I just hate to think of your clubbing those beautiful little martens."

"I don't club them!" Jim pointed out for the hundredth time. "If you like marten so well, I'll bring you in a pair. Fur farms are crazy to get a start on them. If we could raise a few and ship pairs, they might be able to survive."

"We could raise and sell them and you wouldn't have to trap!"

"Maybe," Jim said doubtfully.

A few days later he came home with a live male and female marten. Oddly enough, it was no trouble to haul in the fierce little creatures. From a gunny sack on the ground, they would fight their way out in five minutes; but suspended in a sack, they stayed motionless. Jim put his pair in separate sacks, packed them home on his back, and they never moved.

He had already prepared a cage for them, two stories high—martens are great travelers and need room to run and play—with a wheel for them to play on. The male marten took to the wheel immediately, and would run it for hours without stopping, though the female would jump on and off.

Twenty-four hours later the marten were licking Laurette's fingers and crawling into her lap for food. Like all of the weasel family, martens defile whatever they eat—to keep other animals away from it. When Laurette fed them with a tablespoon, they would eat, then turn and try to get their back ends into the spoon, to fix it for the next fellow. The minute they had eaten, Laurette pushed them off her lap and back into the cage.

The female displayed an annoying wifely habit. When her husband was happily asleep downstairs, she would go up to her bed and within a few minutes sneak back down and wake him. He would obediently get up and go upstairs to the bed she had left. She would curl down in his bed, then a few minutes later, get up, run upstairs and rout him out. When they were sufficiently tame, Laurette let them out of their cage onto the floor, where they wrestled with each other.

More than anything else in their new life, the martens loved cake. When Laurette baked one, they would press their noses against the cage, sniffing and begging so pitifully that she would have to tear off pieces of the warm cake, as it came out of the oven, and feed them.

When Laurette had tamed and trained six pairs of marten, it looked as though her hopes might be realized. There *was* a ready market for marten, and they had no difficulty in selling three pairs to fur farms. They kept three pairs for breeding purposes and applied for a permit to operate a fur farm. But they were turned down because someone had reported that they had killed deer to feed their marten. Actually, the martens' winter diet had consisted of rolled oats, scrap fish caught on a set line in the inlet—and warm cake.

When their permit was rejected, Laurette turned the three pairs loose and sadly resigned herself to the hard fact that Jim must continue to trap and hand-log if they did not want to leave their beloved wilderness.

6

Lady Logger

Worthless old Bob had disappeared, to nobody's great regret, and a deserted Airdale bitch had replaced him. A few days after she came, she had a puppy who was promptly christened Growler because of his knack for making fierce, businesslike sounds long before his wobbly legs could hold him up. Soon after the pup was weaned, the mother, out late at night, was pit-lighted and shot by poachers. But Growler was safe at home and when he was still very young, Jim set about training him.

Almost instinctively he seemed to pick up Jim's reaction to animals. He would lead Jim up to a deer, but never run it. He would become bristly at the smell of a grizzly, but never chase it. He was also valuable as a messenger. He would go miles from the house where Jim was working on the boat, on a lumber boom, or trapping, and bring him home. Or Jim could scribble a note to Laurette, give it to Growler, and the dog would run it back to the cabin.

Growler was most attached to Jim's sharkskin hunting hat, and his fondness for it was the beginning of his early training in retrieving. He carried it for Jim at every opportunity and used it at night for a pillow. When guests arrived, with strange dogs. Growler made no effort to fight the new dog; but he would hurriedly take Jim's hat, run out into the woods, and bury it. Jim would ask Growler to fetch his hat, but Growler played deaf. Jim would repeat the command. Finally, Growler would skulk off into the woods, dig up the hat, and come home with it. Then Jim had to put it on, or Growler would cover it with his body until the other dog went home.

In the spring of 1922 Jim faced a decision. Bartlett and Peterson switched from hand logging to using a donkey engine because it was easier, and they wanted Jim to join them as a full-time partner. But it would have meant a complete change in Jim's way of life—he and Laurette had managed to survive by seasonal work for three years—and they chose freedom again rather than restricted security.

Jim felt that he had had enough experience so that he could, with reasonable safety, go out hand logging alone; with the gas-boat in good working order, he and Laurette could add fishing to his other activities.

He had put in one boom of timber, when Laurette asked if she could join him. She had finished her spring household work and was lonely during the long days while Jim and Growler were off in the woods.

"It's no work for a woman," Jim warned, though privately he was pleased at the idea of her company.

"You used to tell me I was as good in a boat as another man."

"You are," admitted Jim, "better than most. And I don't doubt you could log, too, if you took the notion. But it's dangerous——"

"That," Laurette said firmly, "is why I don't want you doing it alone."

Jim did not spare his new "hand." While he chopped under-cuts into the trees he had selected, he sent Laurette down to the beach to pack up the forty-pound sack which contained the wedges and sledge hammer he would need to wedge the tree over in the right direction.

"That," Jim says today with a twinkle in his blue eyes, "is when you learned to swear."

Quick and impatient, Laurette would start up the mountainside from the beach, carrying the heavy sack. Then, growing weary of the weight, she would try to throw the sack ahead of her, uphill. Invariably, when the heavily laden sack hit, it rolled back down below her, and she would find, with fuming impotence, that she was much worse off than before.

But Laurette took to hand logging like a natural-born woodsman. She was an ideal springboard man because she was not afflicted by dizziness, and her natural grace and rhythm were perfect for the precariously balanced job.

However, there was always work to be done on each tree before Laurette got her chance. The timber Jim selected was big, from four to six feet in diameter. It stood on a 20 per cent grade, which was not steep enough to stump the trees into the water. Therefore, to make certain that the tree, when felled, would not be lost down in the dirt and brush, Jim first felled a couple of "bed trees" crosswise in front of it, for the big tree to fall on. Then he carefully chopped the undercut, and at this point, Laurette crawled onto the springboard, took the other end of the saw, and together they sawed in perfect rhythm until the great tree went over.

Jim's greatest problem was in restraining Laurette. Later in the season when they worked on a section high up in the mountain over a steep bluff, Laurette insisted on climbing on the bluff-side springboard, though it meant standing on a tiny board high in a tree with nothing below but a sheer drop of hundreds of rocky feet down to the shore. It was a spot where few men would have cared to be. Laurette loved it. She found it exhilarating to stand on the very side of the mountain, with the green water five hundred feet below. And then there was the thrill of bracing herself against the trunk and having the tree suddenly go over, crashing to the water, limbing itself as it fell.

One day, however, when Laurette was running the light barking iron over a fallen spruce tree, she worked so fast that her knot of long hair shook free of its pins and tumbled down onto the slippery spruce log. As she tried to shake it back, it stuck—full of fresh spruce pitch. Laurette let out a shriek for help. Jim ran over, laughing as he saw her. But getting her loose was a hair-pulling job. The spruce pitch had matted her hair into a sticky tangle, and for a week Laurette tried coal oil, alcohol, and shampoos. Finally she went up to Jim, a resolute look on her face.

"Get your knife," she ordered, "and chop it all off! I just can't be a woodswoman with long hair."

Jim got out his pocket knife. When he had finished, he looked at her thoughtfully.

"If it doesn't have any knot, or any curl, I think it should have bangs," he decided. "Wait till I get the scissors."

"Go ahead," said Laurette.

Beneath the strangely severe straight hair and the long bangs, Laurette's wide brown eyes suddenly dominated her face, dwarfing her mouth and chin.

"Kind of oriental," Jim decided, "all eyes——"

The proud day they filled their boom with sawn logs, they stopped to listen to a strange sound—a record of "Casey Jones" that filtered across to them from a boat on the other side of the Inlet. Without a word, they grabbed each other and started dancing to the distant tune, their cork boots pounding happily on the boom logs, and Growler jumping around their feet.

However, Laurette never hand logged commercially again. That fall when Jim went to Glendale, he heard the local gossip, which had circulated up and down the Inlet among the summer loggers and fishermen.

"That Stanton," people had been saying; "he can't make a living logging alone, so he's got his woman out doing it."

"This has been the most fun of any season I can remember," Jim said flatly to Laurette, "but I'm never going to let you log again."

Looking at the stubborn Scottish pride in her husband's face, Laurette offered no argument. A man could take so much, after all.

For the next month and a half Jim and Laurette lived on their gas-boat, commercially trolling for coho salmon. They rigged their boat with three 30-foot poles, one in the bow and two amidships, from which hung fishing lines weighted with leads and carrying a total of sixteen to thirty spoons. Each line had a different-toned bell which rang with each catch. They used no bait, just the spoons, and when a fish was hooked they pulled in the line by hand.

The lines were set out each morning at two o'clock, after a quick cup of wake-up coffee. Breakfast was 5 A.M. By ten they were ready for a mug-up of coffee and cakes. Dinner was at twelve, another mug-up at three, with supper at six. They worked until eleven, and then turned in for the night. It didn't take many days of these long hours and the exasperating 2½-m.p.h. speed to make Laurette fidgety and tired. There was no way of getting any real exercise.

The pursuit of the coho took them out of the mouth of the Inlet, where they trolled from cove to cove around Johnstone Strait. But no matter where they were, once each week

Laurette loaded the canoe with her tomcats, Growler, and the dirty laundry, went ashore to get cleaned up for the following week, then paddled back to the gas-boat.

Aboard, she often took over the steering and watched the lines while Jim snoozed. One day when she was running the boat along an unfamiliar bay, there was a low tide and the spoons scraped the bottom, setting all the bells ringing at once, like a church carillon. She ran over and shook Jim.

"Wake up," she shouted. "I've got a fish on every line."

Jim quickly analyzed the situation. "Hell, woman," he yawned, "you've got British Columbia on every line!"

The fish buyer lived on his boat and came around from one fishing boat to another. Pulling in thirty to forty cohoes a day at 75 cents apiece netted them quite a little money that season, but when it was over Laurette delivered an ultimatum.

"I'll gill-net with you, but I never want to troll again. At least we should have our week ends ashore."

Fishing laws stipulated that gill-netting should cease at 6 P.M. each Friday and not commence again until Sunday night at six in order to allow salmon to get through to their spawning grounds.

Gill-netting was done from the boat by suspending a flat net into the water. Nowadays, the large nets are rolled in and out of the boat by pressing a lever. But thirty years or so ago, when Laurette and Jim began gill-netting, their 1,200-foot-long net had to be managed by hand. It took four or five days to learn to handle a net in the boat, and another four or five to learn where to find the fish.

The first few days out each season they always seemed to put the net in the wrong place. It would snag on rocks, ball up with weeds, or float ashore; they would have to pull it back into the boat, get it straightened out, and roll it out again. Usually they fished through the night and slept in the daytime, since the salmon can see the net floating in clear water. But daylight or dark, they had to look at their net every two hours. Caught salmon could die and fall out and sink. Each week the net had to be mended and soaked in a tank of vitrol solution to prevent slime from rotting it. Any hunk of weed or branch of driftwood or brush that might cause a tear had to be carefully untangled.

Of all the odd jobs that attended each occupation—sharpening the saws and axes, cleaning the fishing nets, handling the bait and traps—the most important was overhauling the boat engine. Without the constant use of their boat, all their activities came to an abrupt standstill. And when the engine on the gas-boat or the little kicker engine on the rowboat spluttered and died, they couldn't whistle for help or run to a telephone. They couldn't even buy spare parts.

"If there's one thing a man needs to live in the woods," Jim says with a smile, "I'd say it is to be handy."

7

Chief and Mrs. Kwalate

A colony of Finn trappers had moved onto Malcolm Island, out in Queen Charlotte Strait, between the Inlet and Vancouver Island. They apparently trapped over a wide area, and occasionally Jim and Laurette saw their boats coming into the Inlet. Once when they came abreast of Kwalate, Jim went down to the beach and called to them to come ashore for a visit, but his hospitality was ignored.

Another time when Jim sailed his boat up beside a Finn boat, the cabin door was closed in his face, and the men pulled away. Such incivility in the wilds meant only one thing: they were up to some mischief. Finally Jim found out what it was: the Finns were cruising along the Inlet by Jim's trap line and pit-lighting his mink. They worked at night with carbide lights such as miners use, which they shone along the beach where Jim's traps were set. When the light caught an animal's eyes, they shot it and carried it off. Several times when Jim went out on his mink line, there were no animals. Eventually no traps. And one day Jim saw one of the Finns skinning a mink from which dangled Jim's own trap.

"I've got to get them out of here to protect my line," Jim told Laurette with a worried frown. "But they've got two boats—a double-ended rowboat and a gas-boat—two men and two guns——"

"We're two people, too."

"Well," Jim considered, "I am going to let you go with me, so if I get hurt, you can run the boat. But I don't want them to see you. If I let you go, you'll have to promise to stay out of sight."

That evening, about seven o'clock, they went aboard and without starting the engine let the offshore breeze blow them out into the Inlet. Jim planned to slip up on the pit-lighter, who worked in a rowboat, run him down and capsize his boat, so that his shotgun would be lost and he would be disarmed. They managed to blow softly by without being heard. Jim then started his engine and headed in for the rowboat. The sound of the engine roused both the pit-lighter and his partner in a gas-boat. The rowboat shot ahead and the gas-boat came in from the rear. Jim put on all speed in an effort to overtake the rowboat before the gas-boat caught up with him.

"He's coming up fast," Laurette warned, her eyes straining in the gloom.

"He's got a faster boat," Jim said grimly. "Keep away from the window so he won't see you."

Laurette hid against the wall of the little cabin, and the gas-boat crept closer until it was almost abreast. As it drew alongside, the man at the wheel raised his rifle and aimed at Jim. At that moment Laurette rose up, her face a pale moon in the cabin window. The man switched his aim from Jim to the face at the window, then, apparently changing his mind, threw down his rifle and headed the boat for his partner.

Though the boats were now running abreast, Jim was in line with the rowboat, and as he reached it, he deliberately struck it broadside and rolled it completely over. The trapper went over with his boat, but as he came up, Jim grabbed at him, catching the neck of his shirt in one hand and the coat sleeve in the other. At the same instant the trapper's partner grabbed him. The shirt and coat came off into Jim's boat, but the partner got the man. Then he quickly kicked in the clutch of his fish-box control in the stern of the boat and sped away, with Jim trailing him. As they chased after the speedier boat, Laurette huddled beside Jim.

"He was going to shoot you!" she said indignantly.

"Until he saw you," Jim amended. "When he realized there would be a witness to the murder, he changed his mind."

"I thought for a minute he was going to shoot me, too," Laurette laughed shakily.

"So did I." Jim's voice was taut with anger. "I'm going to turn those rascals in if it's the last thing I do!"

Jim chased the Finns for twenty-five miles but failed to catch up with them.

"Hadn't we better turn back, Jim?" Laurette asked finally. "It's almost daylight now."

"I know he's got a faster boat," Jim admitted, "but I was hoping he'd have engine trouble." He looked around at the lightening early morning sky. "Guess we might as well give up." He switched off the motor and they both listened. Far ahead of them they could hear the gas-boat putt-putting down the Inlet. Reluctantly Jim swung his boat around and they headed home. It was 10 A.M. when they drew into the shore at Kwalate.

"Do you think they'll be back?" Laurette wondered.

"I don't know," Jim said slowly. "But I have a feeling we may be too close to the mouth of the Inlet for safety. There are a lot of poachers and beach tramps down around there."

"How about the head of the Inlet?" Laurette asked. "I'd hate to leave Kwalate, but nobody goes to the Head except the Indians."

"We might give it a look next spring," Jim agreed. "Murder isn't my kind of business."

The area up at the head of Knight Inlet was the wildest part of the region. Jim would get more skins there, and trapping should pay off even when the fur market was low. Too, the flats at the head of the Inlet, formed by deposits from the glacial Klinklini River, were the favorite feeding grounds for grizzlies, who came down out of the mountains to feast off the roots of wild asparagus and wild rhubarb. Jim had seen some of them from a distance the few times he had been up near the Head.

It required no urging for Laurette to help pull up stakes and move further into the wilderness. Her fear of returning to the city was greater than her dislike of trapping. She was always afraid that Jim, feeling responsible for her welfare and safety, would, when things went wrong, insist upon their moving back to Seattle. But once deep in the woods, it is often simpler—however bad things may be—to stay and stick it out rather than turn tail and run. So as more miles separated them from civilization, the happier Laurette would be.

Residence at the Head was a seasonal matter. The coast Indians came there each spring during the oolachan run to make oil out of this cousin of the candlefish and, occasionally, to trap and hunt. During the rest of the year they left their little huts, fish racks, and oil vats to the ravages of the elements.

An experimental German colony had settled at the Head years before and, after trapping out all of the beaver, had finally moved on. The next attempt at living in this isolated wilderness was made by a farmer who had, amazingly enough, tried to raise cattle and to garden. But keeping the big grizzlies away from his stock was more trouble than it was worth.

In the late spring of 1924 Jim and Laurette made an exploratory trip to the Head. Not knowing how long they would be gone, they had ordered supplies for their fall needs as well as for the trip. As usual, there was no money for nonessentials, but Jim made one major purchase, a sixteen-foot Old Town canoe.

They lugged the supplies for the fall into the cabin, loaded those for the trip on the gas-boat, and set out on the twenty-five mile journey to the Head. There they anchored the boat, strapped their packs on, and headed into the valley which lay behind a chain of low hills about two miles from the Klinaklini River. Moving along leisurely, inspecting the country thoroughly, they made camp when darkness fell.

Their way led through a vast, silent, untouched forest. The animal trails looked as though they had been used for centuries. Every few miles they came upon small jewel-like lakes and beaver ponds. The beavers had been mostly trapped out, but to Jim's delight he found a colony of working beavers with fifteen houses. Carefully nurtured, there would be enough beaver so that he could take some each year. And to Laurette's delight, the lakes were teeming with trout. Marten, mink, and otter signs were plentiful. Even more exciting, there were bear trails, bear markings on trees, bear diggings in the meadows, and the giant tracks of the grizzly along the lake shores and the river bank.

After several weeks in the woods, and completely satisfied with the prospects, they worked their way back to the Indian camp on the river. Chief Tom Duncan and his wife Sarah, a former school teacher who spoke English fluently, greeted them cordially. The other Indians whom they had met at the cannery were shy, addressing them as "Chief and Mrs. Kwa-la-te."

When Jim told Tom Duncan of his intention to trap up there, Tom said: "That's my trap line. I inherited it from my father, Chief Humshit."

"In that case," Jim said in disappointment, "I'll trap somewhere else."

"No," Tom said, "you use it. I trapped there with my father until his death. He was a Chilcotin Indian from the interior—a real woodsman. We stayed in the woods and hunted and fished all summer while the rest of the tribe went back to their villages along the coast. Now I trap like the rest—along the river."

"Then no one traps in the interior?"

"Big Louie," Tom said. "He traps up the Klinaklini to Mussel Creek and a mile up the creek."

"I'll stay away from his territory," Jim promised.

Over a cup of tea which Sarah made for them, Tom told how his father and several other adventuresome Indians had killed grizzly bears. They would run along the river in their canoe in the moonlight until they spotted a grizzly fishing from a sand bar. Armed with single-shot 44 rifles and blackpowder cartridges, they left their canoe and went up alongside the bear and made direct shots into the brain, which they had to do to kill it. It was a job the rest of the tribe gladly left to them, even for the seventy-five dollars for which the hides sold at that time.

The Province had recently passed a law permitting the registering of a trap line to keep itinerant trappers away. So Jim registered Chief Tom's with the understanding that he could have it back at any time, if he wished.

The trap line which Jim had in mind at the Head was much longer than the one at Kwalate—it would need four stopover cabins instead of one. The first cabin, similar to the one at Kwalate, they built at Mussel Lake. Then they cleared a ten-mile trail to the beach at the head of the Inlet, where they had left their boat, and weighed anchor for Kwalate.

"You know, Jim," Laurette mused happily, "instead of leaving the woods, as everyone predicted, we're moving in deeper and deeper."

"Do you think," he said, picking up the cue, "that if we came up here and lived in the cabin this winter while I trap, we could make a go of it?"

"It wouldn't be easy," Laurette said. "We'd have to pack in all of our winter supplies."

"I bought the canoe for that. We can tow it behind the gas-boat to the Head, anchor the gas-boat there on the last fall tide where it will be safe until spring, then use the canoe to bring our supplies within a mile of the cabin."

"I'm game," she agreed.

A strange, shabby-looking sailboat was anchored in front of the house at Kwalate. As they drew closer, a dark man and a woman came out on the deck and gestured greetings to them.

"Chief and Mrs. Kwalate," said the man, as they drew alongside, "I am Cheeky Joe and this is my wife. We been here three days waiting out the wind."

Laurette's heart sank. When they had got their supplies at the cannery, they had been told: "Better watch out. There's a bad Indian named Cheeky Joe hanging around. He'll steal anything except a red-hot stove, and if you leave him around long enough for it to cool, he'll take that too." In the unlocked cabin they had left five hundred dollars' worth of supplies, which must see them through the winter.

Jim and Laurette hesitantly invited the Indian couple in for a cup of tea. As they walked up from the beach to the cabin, Laurette noticed that her garden, lush with late summer vegetables, was untouched. Thankfully she saw that everything inside the cabin seemed to be just as they had left it. She hurriedly started a fire in the stove, heated water, and later, over tea and homemade bread and canned venison, the Indians told their story.

While out in their boat fishing, their cabin and everything in it had burned to the ground. The clothes they wore and a few odds and ends in the boat were now all they possessed. They had come to Kwalate to find Jim and then were becalmed when they tried to leave.

"Could we, Chief Kwalate," Joe inquired, "buy a little flours and turnips from you?"

"No," Jim said. "Potlatch. Take what you need as a gift."

The frown on Cheeky Joe's face turned to a grin which spread so wide that, as Jim says, "his ears would have fallen in if he hadn't closed his mouth."

While they talked, Laurette had been quietly loading a box with the "flours," potatoes, canned fruit, tea, sugar, and beans.

"Take turnips and whatever else you need from the garden," she offered.

After they had escorted their guests to the beach, their arms loaded with gifts, Laurette turned to Jim with tears in her eyes.

"Did you see what they were sleeping under? A sail! They were here for three days, with only a handful of smoked fish to eat, with plenty of food and a garden just a few yards away, and they never touched a thing!"

8

Death From the Sky

On the first day of November, with their gas-boat loaded and towing the canoe, Jim, Laurette, the three cats and the dog headed for their new home.

At the Head, on the last high tide, Jim anchored the gas-boat where it would be high and dry until midwinter, and they transferred their supplies—450 pounds—to the canoe. Then with all hands on board, they began the ascent of the treacherous Klinaklini River.

"Running this river in a loaded canoe," Jim said, "means sitting perfectly still with your hair parted in the middle."

The strength of the current made paddling impossible; it was necessary most of the trip for Jim to pole and Laurette to line from the bank. At one point, about a third of the way up, the canoe had to be taken across a sand bar several inches under water. Both of them had to be in the water to do it, with Laurette at the bow and Jim at the stern. As Laurette clambered over the bar to the other side, Jim shot the canoe on to her. To steady it, she stepped off on the other side—and promptly disappeared over her head into deep water. By luck, the canoe swung around in an eddy so that Jim was able to grab it before the current whirled it on to certain destruction downstream. When he had worked it back to safety, he held it with one hand, then reached to help Laurette with the other.

"I could have drowned," she said, spluttering and choking, "for all of you!"

"We would both have died," Jim said calmly, "if we'd lost those provisions."

They finally made the remaining fourteen miles to the bank of the river, where a path led over a 750-foot climb to the cabin. It was a half-hour before dark.

"Let's siwash right here," Jim suggested.

"It's only a mile to the cabin," Laurette said.

"But it's a rough mile," Jim protested, "and we can't make it before dark."

"Mussel Lake or bust," Laurette said stubbornly. "We can leave our supplies here until morning—the cabin is stocked. I'll take along a pot and some coffee."

She started up the trail, the tomcats and dog following behind. With a quick glance to make sure that the canoe and their supplies were safely up on the bank, Jim followed. By the time they had made it halfway up the steep, zigzagging trail, darkness had set in. To make matters worse, a soft but steady rain began to fall. Jim now took the lead. To add to their misery, the cats and the dog began mewing and whining plaintively. When total darkness set in, Jim had to admit that he was hopelessly lost. Gropingly he took a step forward, and plunged over a twenty-foot drop.

"Are you hurt?" Laurette cried out in fright.

"Not much," he replied, scrambling back up to her. "I landed in some bushes. We're lost. I don't even know where the river is. We'll have to stop right where we are until morning."

Fumbling around on the ground close by, he gathered enough fir twigs to start a fire, added more and more, and then piled on larger chunks. As the flames rose in the wet, dark night, the cats and dog crawled closer and closer, preempting most of the warmth. Laurette sank down wearily and tried to remove her sodden boots, but pull as she might, even with Jim's help, they would not come off. Her wet, sore feet had swollen until the boots were tighter than her skin.

"What's for supper?" Jim asked, managing a grin.

"Coffee and cigarettes."

There was nothing to do except huddle as close to the fire as possible and keep it as high as they dared. It was their only protection from the wild animals around them. Along toward midnight, they heard the howl of timber wolves. Little by little, it came nearer and nearer, but Jim kept the fire blazing. Shortly after midnight the rain turned to snow.

When daylight came, nearly a foot of snow had fallen. Putting out their fire, the miserable little party worked their way back to the trail and down to the river bank. There Jim started another fire and set up the fly while Laurette made a pot of coffee and heated a can of stew, which they shared with the animals. Then she and Jim crawled under the little tent and went to sleep.

They slept all that day and night, and only awoke the following day when the cats and the dog insisted on being fed. Then they packed into the cabin without trouble, and while Laurette put their new home in order, Jim went back for another load. It took him four days, making two trips a day, to pack in their supplies. All of that time it rained during the day and snowed each night.

At last Jim was ready to set his traps. However, with the soft snow covering everything, he was unable to get them out. Nor was it possible to extend the trail for the trap line and build the other stopover cabins. Laurette's problems were almost as difficult. Without a stove, she had to do her cooking in the fireplace. Furthermore, with the snow constantly coming down so early in the season, it appeared that they well might run out of supplies. To conserve what they had brought, Laurette went to Mussel Lake each day and caught trout; the first day she caught thirty in less than half an hour with a barb filed off her hook. Jim built a smoke rack, just an extension of cedar shakes on the chimney, so they could smoke the fish the way the Indians did. As Laurette caught fish, she opened them, took out the backbone, and later strung them over the chimney to smoke and dry. In two weeks they turned parchment yellow and kept indefinitely.

Having plenty of fish to eat did not, however, eliminate their other problems. In thirty days of miserable rainy, snowy weather, Jim was able to trap only four marten.

"I need more time to study where the animals go in this kind of weather," he told Laurette.

One night, after a month in the woods, as they were preparing for bed, they were electrified by a thunderous crash outside. Their cabin was placed in a grove of giant Douglas firs, many of them a hundred and fifty to two hundred feet high. The increasing weight of the constantly falling snow, held in the tops by their evergreen branches, became so great that it had toppled a tree to the ground. As they listened, there was another terrifying crash.

"Don't undress!" Jim ordered firmly. "If one hits the cabin and doesn't kill us, we'll try to make it to the river." Hurriedly he doused out the fire. "If a tree traps us," he explained, "we don't want to be burned alive!"

The rest of the long night they sat huddled on the edge of the bunk, the cats and the dog at their feet, as the big trees kept falling. Three . . . four . . . five . . . a seeming eternity between each crash . . . six . . . seven. It seemed certain that one of the giant trees would hit the cabin. Eight . . . nine . . . ten. The cats and dog huddled closer. Eleven . . . twelve . . . thirteen.

Then came daylight.

They went outside and counted the fallen firs— Thirteen immense trees, crisscrossed in such a way that it was a miracle the cabin hadn't been crushed.

"I'll never again believe that thirteen is an unlucky number," Laurette said.

"A couple of them just barely missed the cabin," Jim observed. "We've got to get out of here fast."

"It was the longest night of my life."

"And mine," he agreed. "Let's get going."

Though it was an almost insuperable job packing their supplies through four feet of snow to the river, desperation drove them on. They made two trips a day, spending their nights on the river bank to avoid being trapped in the cabin. As the weather turned colder, Laurette stayed at the river to keep the fire going. On his last trip Jim staggered out of the Mussel Lake cabin with three 50-pound soldered food tins. They didn't dare leave any food, not knowing where they might have to spend the rest of the winter.

There was reason to hurry. The back eddies of the river were already frozen over solid, and the river itself was beginning to freeze. As they pushed off, with all hands and supplies aboard, Jim had to break a crust of ice on the river with his paddle to get the canoe out into the current.

Fortunately going down was not as difficult as the trip up. By noon they came out of the Klinaklini to the Head where their gas-boat was high and dry on the bank. It would be another thirty days, according to the tide table, until there was a tide high enough to launch it.

"But I don't care," Jim said. "I'd rather we stayed here on the boat than get our heads smashed in the woods."

They put up their fly on the stern to make an extra room so that all of their activities would not be cramped in the little cabin of the boat.

Cooking was again a problem because the little twelve-by fourteen-boat stove had no oven. Jim dug a hole in the bank and filled it with live coals from the stove, on which Laurette placed her Dutch oven. By throwing coals on top of it as well, she was able to make bread and roast wild goose. Wilderness or no wilderness, she saw that they ate well—when food was available.

A month later the tide came, and they pushed off for Kwalate in a bitter winter storm.

At the end of the winter—lived mostly under constant danger and on the thin edge of starvation, the trapping had netted them only forty dollars.

"That's the most work I ever did," Jim said somberly, "for so little money."

"It hardly seems worth it," Laurette added with a deep sigh.

"But we've got to make a living somehow; and everything we've tried has gone wrong."

"Including the trapping, Jim."

"Yes," he agreed. "But I still think I can make money in furs, once I get going. There are more animals at the Head than anywhere else; and I'm all for moving back as soon as we can."

Laurette remembered that the farther from civilization they were, the better the chance of their staying in the north woods.

Besides, what with lumber camps and summer visitors, Kwalate was getting too crowded for them.

"I'm with you, Jim," she said.

When the spring thaws came in March, and Jim went to Glendale, he learned that a fisherman had taken a couple of men to the Head and left them there. This news worried him and as soon as the weather cleared, he went to the Head alone and on up the trail to the cabin. There he found utter desolation. Everything had been wantonly destroyed. The beaver houses had been dynamited and their inhabitants killed, and his cabin ransacked. The food from his cache which the poachers had not been able to eat or carry away, they had thrown out. The cabin itself had been stripped of its furnishings and the door smashed. Jim lifted his arms to the heavens and cursed loudly. Then he realized that it wasn't nature which had ruined him—but man.

He turned in a report to the Mounties and every effort was made to apprehend the poachers. The only possible way they could have left the region was through the wild Klinaklini canyon to the interior, a seventy-five-mile trip that only a few Indians had been known to make. The poachers were never caught and Jim doubted that they survived.

Trappers had told Jim that muskrats multiplied rapidly in this country. With the beaver gone, he ordered a dozen rats from an animal farm in the Peace River country. If he had any luck he would have thousands of rats to trap in three or four years. Prime skins were bringing four dollars apiece.

He hand-logged during the summer, making just enough money to pay for their winter's supplies. When the muskrats arrived at Glendale the end of August, he made a hurried trip to collect his new stock. One glance at the dull-eyed animals, packed in a three-by six-foot sheet-iron cage, convinced Jim he must rush them to the lakes before they died, so he and Laurette placed the cage aboard their gas-boat and high-tailed it for the head of the Inlet. Although it was already dark, Jim lashed the iron cage onto his pack-board, Laurette carried their bedroll and a little food, and they set out for Long Lake, four miles through the woods. It took them seven hours to cover the rough trail to the lake bank, where Jim turned the rats loose.

Late in September he went back to his trap line alone, determined to find out why, in addition to the bad weather, he had been so unsuccessful the winter before. Perhaps he had been trapping too low down on the mountainside. He built four miles of tortuous trail at an altitude of nine hundred to thirteen hundred feet and set his traps there. Although the weather was good, and he ran the line religiously, it netted him even less than the forty dollars he had earned the year before.

"A trapper," he often told Laurette, "must study his territory as a fisherman learns where to fish. I know the animals are there, but I haven't learned where to set my traps for them."

The following spring and summer Jim hand-logged three sections but no buyers appeared; he heard that a sharp drop in prices had upset the business. Loggers were, as one of them put it, down to a diet of "clams and corn meal." It looked as though he and Laurette were really up against a stone wall this time. He sent the logs into Vancouver on the chance that they might sell, borrowed a hundred dollars from a logger friend, and bought only the absolute necessities. Where the money for their winter order would come from was in the laps of the gods.

"I guess we're starved out," he said to Laurette with finality. "I don't know where to turn any more."

"You know, Jim," she said fancifully, ignoring the significance of his statement, "what I'd really like to have right now is a great big, juicy watermelon!"

Later in the day they heard the putt-putt of a motor and, in the distance, saw the Fish Warden's boat heading their way. He came ashore, carrying in his arms a big watermelon, which he handed to Laurette.

"You have fed me so many times," he said, "I thought I'd bring you something you can't get in these parts."

After they had eaten it and the Warden had gone on his way, stuffed full of not only watermelon but waffles, Jim turned to her.

"Dear," he asked dryly, "why didn't you wish for a million dollars?"

9

Yachting in the Wilderness

Laurette's wish coming true proved to be a turning point in their luck. The logs sold for enough to pay off Jim's hundred-dollar debt, with just enough left over to buy a minimum supply of provisions for the winter. He had a good season trapping and, as a result, in the spring of 1927 prospects were a little brighter.

Year by year, as Jim and Laurette clung to the Inlet, Jim's reputation as a woodsman had spread. The Mounties, the fish and game wardens, and the forest rangers not only considered the Stantons good settlers who believed in the conservation of wildlife and natural resources; they also passed on the word that if anyone wanted to know anything about the region to ask "that fellow Stanton."

The first result of this free—but well-earned—publicity came when Melville Dollar, of the Dollar Steamship Line, brought his yacht into the Inlet to fish, and one of the Mounties told him to use Jim as a guide.

"Jim Stanton knows those woods and streams," he asserted, "like the back of his hand."

Jim proved to be exactly the kind of guide Dollar wanted, and he went back to the States praising not only the fishing but Jim as well.

"Trout like you have never seen," he said enthusiastically to his friends. "Wild, unexplored country. Real glacial water. But be sure to get hold of that fellow Stanton. He'll take you where the fish are."

A long line of pleasure boats began heading toward Knight Inlet. There were British, Welsh, and American boats, and many of them hired Jim as a guide.

On one trip with an aristocratic Englishman, Jim found grizzly tracks and led the party into the forest until they saw him.

"I want that trophy," the Englishman exclaimed. "Let's leave some food for him, and perhaps he will be around tomorrow."

Sometime later Jim killed a two-hundred-pound hair seal and, with the help of some of the crew from the yacht, securely roped it to a log, twelve feet long and ten inches in diameter, so heavy it took three men to lift it. But next morning, both the seal and the log were gone. Careful examination showed that the bear had dragged them—Jim estimated that the two weighed over eight hundred pounds—for a short way and had then picked them up in his powerful arms and carried them off. Jim trailed the bear into the woods for two days but found no trace of the seal, the rope, the log, or the grizzly. A few days later, however, he again spotted the giant, and his hunter was able to bag him. That grizzly was one of the largest ever taken out of the territory; the hide measured ten feet six inches both in length and width.

Of all the yachts entering the Inlet, the one that particularly interested the Stantons was the *Surprise*, which came in June, 1927, and remained until September. Formerly owned by King Leopold of Belgium, it was one of the most luxurious and magnificent pleasure craft afloat in those days. The overall length was 255 feet; it had a tonnage of 1,350, and carried a crew of sixty-five. The formal service included silver settings for 225 people, and part of the crew doubled as an orchestra, playing during the dinner hour. The yacht was then owned by a Welsh steamship and silver mine magnate who carried on his business by wireless with his many enterprises.

Soon after the *Surprise* had anchored off the Stantons' cabin, a launch brought the Welshman ashore. A taciturn, dynamic man, he developed an immediate fondness for Jim and Laurette. After visiting with them a few moments and discussing the possibilities of fishing on the Inlet, he invited them for dinner aboard his yacht.

From their Kwalate cabin to formal dinner, with service plates and a French chef, was a violent change of pace for the Stantons. Laurette managed to restore a navy-blue silk dress —brought from Seattle eight years before—plastered her wild bangs neatly in place, and hoped for the best. Jim dug around in old gear until he found his one business suit, and pressed it sketchily between mattress and bed springs.

The service was completely formal, presided over by a butler in tails and four waiters, but there was no evidence that their impeccably groomed host was disturbed by the somewhat casual wear of his guests.

"Will your wife be with you soon?" Jim inquired.

"Next week," the Welshman replied resignedly. "She's in Victoria now. We shall need your services, Mr. Stanton. She is bringing guests, and we shall want a fishing trip. The crew is at your disposal."

Jim was hired to come aboard and serve as guide. Though he ate in the mess with the stewards, he was assigned a stateroom—and a valet. The first morning he awoke on shipboard and saw a little "hammered down" man standing over him with a silver tray containing hot milk and coffee.

"Who are you?" Jim demanded.

"Your valet, Mr. Stanton. You may call me Boojie. Here is your coffee, sir. How would you like your bath?"

Jim rose in the bunk, clutching the bedclothes around him. "What do you mean, how would I like it?"

"The temperature, sir," Boojie said patiently. "Hot or cold?"

"Hot," ordered Jim. "Hot as hell." He lay back in bed, listening luxuriously to the sound of running water. It had been years since he had a piping hot bath. Boy, he wished he could take one home to Laurette!

When he came back from fishing, wet and tired, he found clean clothes laid out on his bunk, a hot bath drawn and waiting. In the morning his dirty fishing clothes would appear—freshly laundered. All through that summer Jim luxuriated in a life he had never known—and would never know again.

Though he was paid for full-time service during the three months that the yacht lay in the Inlet, Jim was allowed to go ashore whenever he wasn't needed. He had only to commandeer one of the speedboats for a few days. Sometimes the Welshman came along too—to visit the Kwalate cabin and pay his respects to Laurette.

Jim's most arduous assignment of the season was to take the Welshman and his wife, their daughter, and guests on a fishing trip. Jim selected the Handwaddie, a clear-water stream eight miles from Kwalate, which he knew abounded with fine fish. He picked a campsite two miles up the river from the Inlet, and there, under his direction, the crew set up an oasis in the wilderness, complete with Coleman lights and tables and benches overhung with canvas. Even a bathtub was set up that took four men to install. The cooks and stewards, and those of the crew who were needed to maintain the camp, brought the total to twenty-seven people.

The Welshman had purchased a 21-foot-long Hudson Bay freighting canoe to use on the river, and as soon as camp was set up, it was Jim's job to take him and his wife and their daughter fishing. The Welshman took the bow, where he expected to flycast; his daughter sat in the middle, with a trolling line, and his wife chose the stern, where she intended to bait fish.

As Jim began poling the canoe along the river, the Welshman called out, "Hold it, Stanton, we are approaching fish. Don't run over them!"

When Jim dutifully slowed the canoe, the daughter, amidships, cried, "Damn it, Stanton, my spoon is sinking to the bottom. Move on."

While Jim alternately poled, then slowed down, the wife, sitting in the stern beside him, turned to glare at Jim. "Get to a place where I can find a fish," she demanded. "Quit fooling around!"

After the four-week Handwaddie trip, they moved back to the yacht. Jim spent a few days at home with Laurette, then reported back for duty.

As the yacht slowly cruised the ninety miles of Inlet Waters, Jim would mention likely fishing grounds, and the Welshman would say, "Get me a sample, Stanton." At night, after dinner, the "sample" fish would be brought on a silver platter for inspection. If it was not to his liking, he would say, "No matter," and Jim was dismissed for the evening. But if he approved, he would say, "Stanton, would you care to make me a path?"

The next morning Jim would take thirty of the crew, with their English hatchets, and set out for shore. There he led the men by blazing the trail ahead, and they followed, chopping the clearance. "The easiest trail-making I ever did," Jim declared.

As the time came for the *Surprise* to move on, the Welshman called Jim in.

"I like you, Stanton," he said, "and I want to keep you in my employ."

"I've enjoyed working for you," Jim said amiably.

"I've decided to take you and Mrs. Stanton with us," the Welshman announced. "When we reach England, you can become manager of one of my estates. I will pay you well."

For a long minute Jim studied the strange man he had learned to admire. The offer was tempting—a long sea voyage on a royal yacht, a permanent job in beautiful surroundings, and good pay the year around.

In an instant of flashing memory he thought of many things: of the long, hard winters snowbound in their cabin with barely enough food to sustain them until spring; of the many lonesome days and nights he had spent on his trap line; of Laurette balanced high on a bluff-side springboard, pulling away energetically at her end of the crosscut saw until the giant tree was felled; of the agonizing night they spent in the cabin up at the Head while the tall Douglas firs crashed all about them; of the grizzlies . . .

"I'm very sorry, sir," Jim said quietly, "but we belong here."

When the *Surprise* swept majestically out of the Inlet, it left two tangible mementoes behind. The yacht had carried several pianos, which no one ever played. Jim asked if he might buy one of them, and the Welshman agreed. Later, listening to Laurette play and hearing her still lovely voice, Jim did not regret the purchase he could so ill afford.

At the same time, a gift was sent to Laurette. Its name was Dennis—or Miss Dennis, a hairless tropical pig which had been presented to the Welshman by a South Sea Island queen. In the South Sea Islands, pigs, brought to the islands by British whaling ships, were considered priceless possessions.

Dennis had been treated as a treasured pet aboard the *Sur-*

prise. One of the crew had been assigned to her as a valet, and she was given a bath and manicure daily. Born in a tropical climate, she had grown no protective hair, and her hide was velvety tan with a few dark spots.

Laurette patted the immaculate, smooth hide. "Oh, Jim, what will we do with her? She'll freeze this winter, and we can't keep her in the cabin with us!"

For once Jim was of little help. "I don't know," he shrugged. "I suppose we could give her to someone who'd have the nerve to slaughter her."

"I'll slaughter you!"

Jim was not to be indifferent to Dennis for long. As he and Laurette walked back to the cabin, Dennis trotted happily at their heels, like a puppy. When they went in the door, she stood on the sill and squealed.

"Guess she wants to come in," Jim said.

"She wants to be invited in," corrected Laurette. "Come in, Dennis."

A little later, after Laurette had made a pot of tea, Dennis walked over to the table and squealed again, expectantly.

"What does she want this time—a cup of tea?" Jim asked.

"I guess so." Laurette poured some tea into a small saucer and set it on the floor. Dennis tasted it, looked up reproachfully, and squealed again.

"She's a British-trained pig," Jim laughed. "She wants milk and sugar!"

Laurette picked up Dennis's dish of tea, added a spoon of sugar and some canned cream, and set it back. Dennis put her snout into it, sipped, glanced up at them with a contented grunt, then went happily back to her tea.

"Well I'll be damned!"

Though Dennis's vocabulary was limited to squeals of displeasure and grunts of satisfaction, they soon felt the influence of her personality. She was spoiled, loving, and playful. She made friends of the rather startled Growler and the tomcats, and when Laurette or Jim started down a trail, she would fall in line, single file, along with Growler and the tomcats. She always trailed going into the woods, but once the direction was reversed and they were on their way home, Dennis would scramble ahead, and fight Growler for the lead position.

As the cold winds blew up around the Inlet, Laurette worried about her new pet. One day she came out on the beach where Dennis and the cats were playing, and felt the pig's slender, chilly legs.

"Come along, Miss Dennis, we've got to do something about you."

Obediently Dennis followed and when they were back in the cabin, Laurette reached up into the rafters and pulled out two pairs of knee-length wool socks.

"Come here, Dennis," she said invitingly.

Dennis walked up to Laurette and watched with interest as her mistress picked up one slim leg and pulled on a sock. When Laurette put that hoof down, Dennis voluntarily offered the next one. She seemed highly pleased with her four warm wool socks, and scampered around the room as if showing them off.

When snow came, Laurette put a barrel out on the beach and loaded it with wild hay. Here Dennis slept in comparative comfort.

An excellent swimmer, Dennis squealed to go along every time Jim started the boat. He had only to pull alongside a boomstick and say, "All right, Dennis," and the little pig would clamber aboard. He rigged up a fly on deck in the stern, and Dennis slept under it.

It was more difficult to get her out. When they were coming ashore, Jim would say, "Overboard, Dennis." Dennis would squeal protestingly, but at his repeated command she would scramble over the side, hit the water with a shudder, and swim ashore.

If the boat left without her, Dennis would swim out into the water and trail it for a while before giving up. Then when she heard the distant sound of the motor, she would dive in and swim out to meet the boat.

One day Jim and Laurette went to Glendale. They took Growler along but made Dennis stay at home. While they were gone, a fish warden, who was a heavy drinker, stopped at Kwalate for a visit. Dennis heard the boat coming, hopped into the water, and swam out to meet it. The two tomcats, who had been playing with her on the beach, trailed after her.

A few days later a pale, very sober fish warden came back to Kwalate.

"Do you," he asked Jim fearfully, "have a pig that swims?"

"That's right," said Jim.

"And cats that go into water?"

"Yes, we do."

"Well!" the fish warden sighed with relief. "I guess I won't have to go on the wagon after all!"

Dennis had only one bad habit. She had reached that uneasy, titillating period of girlhood when everything male excited her. All strange men who came near the Stantons were subject to her embarrassing demonstrations. She would nudge them, nuzzle, gurgle small pleasantries, and rub against their legs.

She developed such a crush on one government man that she would swim out to meet his boat, which she easily recognized, and swim around and around it, squealing happily as he came ashore. When the poor man landed, she would crowd against him and snort her song of love. He complained to Jim.

"You know, dear, after all," Jim said to Laurette when he had left, "we can't lose our friends on account of Dennis. You'll have to admit, it's rather frightening to have a pig making love to you——"

"She needs a mate," Laurette said sadly.

"That would really put us in the pig business!"

"Well," Laurette said, "we might as well be. We've got her—and you know you haven't the heart to kill her."

"All right, all right." Jim shook his head. "We'll have a pig farm along with everything else——"

So the Stantons became the owners of a Yorkshire boar named Bill. When he arrived on order at Kwalate, Bill was a snow-white husky baby of three months. The fact that he was not yet old enough to mate was immediately obvious to Dennis, who sniffed at him disdainfully. But she stopped bothering men, apparently deciding to bide her time and raise Bill to suit herself. The young Yorkshire was even-tempered and immediately devoted to his future wife, although she bossed him unmercifully. However, his first week on the Inlet, Bill managed to escape her supervision.

A logging friend of Jim's, with an eye on the cold, unsociable winter which lay ahead, had suggested that he and Jim do a little home-brewing on a fifty-fifty basis.

The beer-making proved successful, the logger went on his way with his share, and Jim went back to working on his boat. Little Bill, rooting around inquisitively, came upon the sediment left from the brewing, which the men had poured out on the ground not far from the cabin. The flavor appealed to him. He sucked deeper and deeper, happily swilling up all of it.

Back at the cabin, when Dennis came in for a cup of tea,

Laurette noticed that Bill was not trailing her. Growler and the cats were out on the beach, but Bill was not in sight.

"Jim," she called anxiously, "Bill's missing. Have you heard any wolves around?"

Jim left his work and hurried up to the cabin. They searched everywhere. When Dennis heard them calling, she also took up the hunt. Suddenly Jim straightened up: "Listen to that."

From a thicket a little way down the beach came a contemptuous snort. There was Dennis, her snout up in ladylike disapproval, while little Bill, weaving and apologetic, tried to make up to her. Just as they came up, Bill collapsed. His little pink eyes closed and he fell fast asleep.

"Is he sick?" Laurette said in alarm.

Jim walked over to Bill and lifted the pig's head. Bill's eyes didn't open; at the touch of Jim's hand he merely grunted and began to snore. Jim sniffed the escaping fumes from his mouth.

"He's drunk!" he announced. "He's really got a load on."

"Well," Laurette laughed, "I guess there's nothing we can do but let him sleep it off."

"That's right," Jim agreed. "He's close enough to the house; I don't think the wolves will get to him."

"Besides, he's got a guard." Laurette nodded to Dennis.

Dennis had taken up the vigil. At a fastidious distance from Bill, she settled down to await his recovery.

10

Grizzly Country

When the wolves did come to Kwalate, in January, 1928, they did not come for pigs. They were after Growler. Jim had tried to train Growler never to follow a wolf call, and, with Jim, Growler would not run a wolf in the woods. He seemed to understand the danger. But Growler was a healthy young male, and none of Jim's training proved strong enough to overcome the lure of the bitch wolves.

Early one morning when Laurette opened the cabin door for Growler to go outside, he shot through the door and headed straight for the woods.

"Jim," Laurette called sharply, "something's wrong. Growler's going to the woods instead of the beach."

Jim called the dog, who was now a streak of brown in the distance and though Jim shouted, Growler didn't even turn his head.

"It's the wolves!" Jim said anxiously. "Get my big coat, Laurette." He pulled on his heavy wool shirt and high trapping boots, slipped into the coat Laurette held for him, picked up his gun, and headed out into the cold morning in the direction Growler had disappeared, quietly cursing himself for not having heard the wolves in the night and kept Growler inside.

January is the mating season for the Siberian wolves. The bitches, sneaking up near the cabin at night, had called to Growler, luring him out to meet them. The dog wolves, secreted in the forest, stayed back, letting the females lure their prey.

Jim trailed Growler all that day. The wolves were moving in a radius of two or three miles from the cabin; he could hear their howls in the distance and sometimes distinguish Growler's lusty bark. At night Jim came home weary. Though he had been close enough to call to Growler, the dog had not come to him. Next morning he ate a quick breakfast and headed out again.

For a second day Jim trailed the wolves. He never caught them, nor was he able to separate Growler from the pack. Growler had joined the females and was running with them. The dog wolves had so far let him alone because of the strong human scent on him.

The third morning Jim found Growler. The dog lay not fifty yards from the cabin, which he apparently had been trying to reach. He was still alive—but he was slashed to ribbons. The hundred-pound dog-wolves had finally attacked, and had left no part of Growler's body unscathed. Jim didn't try to carry the dog to the cabin, for it was too late to do anything. He simply sat with Growler and held his head until he died.

Jim had always hated the wolves, but so far he had had no success in his sporadic efforts to hunt or trap them. Now he made up his mind to deliberately wage war on them, and kill every one that he could.

However, killing wolves, as Jim knew, was not a simple matter. The wariest animal in the wilds, the big wolves have not only the keenest eyesight and the keenest scent of any animal in the woods but also a sixth sense, a sort of extrasensory power, which warns them of danger long before other animals are aware of it.

It is almost impossible to stalk them, and no ordinary trap will catch a wolf. The only thing that Jim had known the clever rascals to take was a water set. Despite the cold January weather, Jim got ready, that day of Growler's death, to set water traps for the wolves.

When he had placed his traps, he splashed water over the bait to wash away all human scent. Then he waded along in the water, far from the set, so there would be no human scent on the bank near the traps.

That night Jim was lucky. Three of the big dog-wolves were trapped and—for the first time in his life—Jim found a lustful joy in killing.

Jim's reputation as a guide spread slowly—he continued to fish and hand-log as well as trap—and by the fall of 1928 he had managed to put away two hundred dollars more than they needed for the winter's supplies. It wasn't much and the saving hadn't been easy. It had been done not by earning a lot, but rather by spending only a little. In nearly a decade of hardship and privation, they had indulged in but two luxuries: the landscape window and the piano.

Now it would be safe to make the move from Kwalate to the head of the Inlet, close to what, in spite of numerous set-backs. Jim still hoped would be a really profitable trapping area. The previous year, on one of several trips to his trap line there, he had found two trappers living in a one-room alder log house two miles up the slew from the salt water. They had settled in to poach on Jim's registered line. Jim had run them off and, by so doing, had acquired the cabin. With a dwelling already built, and money enough for necessary improvements, the time had come to move into the grizzly country.

They loaded the gas-boat with food, gear, pigs, and cats—and the piano. Jim skidded the piano onto a fishing skiff, which he had built the year before, and made it fast with blocks. Since he had calculated their move so that they would arrive on high tide, he could then tow the piano almost to the door of the new cabin, which sat at tide-level on the flats at the head of the Inlet.

Only one thing marred Jim's careful optimism about their new home. Not long before they left Kwalate, he had met a police boat in Glendale and learned that a Finn trapper, seventy-five miles in the interior, had gone berserk and killed a man, then killed the policeman who went after him.

"Last report," the officers told Jim, "he had a 22 rifle, a 30-30, ammunition, blankets, and food, and was heading over the coastal range, which would bring him out near your new place."

Jim finally decided against telling Laurette. He believed the murderer would stick to the woods rather than risk capture on the open beach, but the knowledge of an armed criminal loose in the forest put him on constant guard. As he jogged along the trails, he kept his eyes peeled for a man's tracks, searching the sand bars, mud banks, and any soft ground that would show a footprint. When he reached one of his cabins, he crept up on a hill above, where he could study it for signs of habitation: heat waves in the air or smoke from the chimney. He waited until dark, then sneaked down and lay against the cabin wall to listen before going in.

Jim never met the murderer, and concluded that the man had struck either the Klinaklini or Franklin glaciers and died.

"I just lost my nerve," he admitted later to Laurette. "I think it's as bad an experience as a man can have, to keep going in the woods knowing there is a crazed murderer around."

"I know," she said, "I was scared, too. One of the Indians told me, but I didn't want to worry you."

Jim's new trap line took eight days to run, and along it there were four cabins. The country was so wild that only years later did he discover, by aerial photograph, that there were four more lakes within a mile of his regular run which he had never seen as well as the seven lakes he knew about. The forest trees were enormous. The firs and spruce ran up to ten feet in diameter, and there were cedars which measured twenty-seven feet around. In one hollow giant cedar Jim had made a stopover camp.

The interior of the tree measured six by eight feet, and was hollow up to thirty feet. A dead hemlock, which had grown nearby, was encompassed by the big tree, and its hollow trunk formed a natural chimney. Jim built a rock fireplace under the hemlock chimney, and fashioned a doorway for his hideout by covering the entrance with his silk fly. A little spring under one of the roots furnished fresh water. With his sleeping bag across from the fireplace, and a stump for a chair just inside the tent flap, it was such a cozy and enchanting place—that is, after his fear of the madman had passed— that Jim used it year after year.

He even had company in one of his cabins: deer, or jumping, mice, light brown in color, with kangaroo-type hind legs and little white vests. Their tails were as long as their bodies, and they could jump a foot in the air from any angle. Jim fed them, and they entertained him at night by jumping around the cabin, leaping at sudden, crazy angles. "They looked like fireworks going off," Jim says.

When Jim crawled into his sleeping bag, one brave young mouse tried to make a nest in his hair. Jim gently brushed him away, but the mouse came back, and lay quietly against the top of Jim's head.

Whenever Jim came to the cabin, the mouse was waiting for him. For three winters this same mouse lived in the cabin and greeted Jim every time he came through. "You know,"

Jim told Laurette, "it gave me a pleasant feeling, when I was jogging along alone over eight or ten miles of trail through the lonesome forest, to know that something alive would welcome me at night."

That fall Laurette too made a few friends. One afternoon when she was playing the piano, she suddenly sensed an audience. Turning around, she saw that four frogs had found their way up through a knothole in the cabin floor and were sitting in a line beside her, watching her play. As long as she played, they were motionless, but when she stopped, they hopped back down the knothole. The next day the same thing occurred. For weeks the frog audience arrived promptly whenever Laurette played. They were so tame that she could touch them; and she found that if she stroked them a certain way, a sound strangely like singing came from their thrumming throats.

Despite the strain of working in the woods with a killer at large, Jim had taken a lot of pelts. His marten traps down by Mussel Creek had yielded a phenomenal three or four marten to the mile, proving that they went down instead of up in cold weather. He would know from now on where to set traps for them. The muskrats had multiplied, their customary fashion, from the original pair to an estimated eighteen hundred to two thousand rats. But it was the same old story: the skins that had brought $4 apiece when Jim introduced the rats were now down to 25 cents. And the older males were busily driving the younger ones off, so that they migrated out of Jim's area. Eventually a strange disease hit the remaining rats, causing their joints to loosen, and all but a few died. However, his venture paid off when the prime interior mink, which usually migrated in cold weather, leaving only a coarse-haired beach mink in the area, stayed around to live off the rats, and netted Jim $19 a skin.

Tantalizing evidence of grizzlies was all around them, but those not hibernating kept away from human scent. Not far from their cabin was a 150-foot spruce tree with a natural crotch-seat in the top. Jim climbed this lookout tree whenever he could, but it was not until spring that his vigil was rewarded. As the bears came out of hibernation, and became accustomed to the new smell and disassociated it from danger, they began to drift back to their normal feeding grounds in the flats surrounding the cabin. From his perch Jim was able to observe the bears for miles around, frequently seeing as many as twelve grizzlies at one time, and during July, when the mother bears were out feeding along with their cubs, he counted forty.

Soon he was able to identify thirty individual bears by sight. Five of these fed regularly within a mile of the cabin. As the grizzlies became increasingly familiar with the Stantons, four of them made beds within a hundred yards of the house. When they got up from these day beds at two or three o'clock in the afternoon they would come up to the cabin and stand around for a while. Then in the cool of the afternoon they would amble down into the field and dig for wild rhubarb roots, a plant which grows like a parsnip with a dozen thick, rootlike fingers in the earth. With a single swipe of a paw, the bears would dig out the plant, roots and all, and eat it. Two or three of these clusters provided enough sustenance for six or eight hours. When the grizzlies had eaten, they began to play. The young bears, invariably curious, prankish and playful, wrestled, picked up sticks and rocks and tossed them in the air, and continually investigated everything new and interesting.

Later, perhaps, they would all go into the water of the slew and play. Eleven o'clock seemed to be the general bedtime, and Jim and Laurette, from their own bunk in the cabin, could hear the snoring and heavy breathing of their grizzly neighbors.

As with their cats, dogs, and pigs, the Stantons soon learned the different voices of the grizzlies. The babies, like all babies, cried. Little, and sometimes big ones, too, might whine. Then there was the adult bear's growl which sounded like an angry snarl.

One day, in the early afternoon, Laurette and Jim heard a pitiful whine. They went outside, following the cry, and came upon a sow grizzly with "this year's cub" down at the slew. The mother had crossed the water, but baby bear was on a little log, protesting piteously, while his mother ran up and down the bank—thirty feet of water away from him—urging him in. He was crying, Laurette remarked to Jim, "like a baby with a safety pin sticking in him." When he saw the Stantons coming toward him, he jumped into the slew and swam to his mother. As he reached her, she "said something to him," her snout against his ear, and then they ambled off into the woods.

Fascinating and delightful though it was to have grizzlies in their back yard, Laurette did not enjoy having them in her garden. Although the bears were not interested in eating the vegetables, they had no compunction about walking on them. Wherever one of those mammoth paws fell, it drove the plant beneath it into the ground. "When a bear steps on a hill of potatoes," Jim said, "he sets it back two weeks." One garden which Laurette had hopefully nursed had to be completely abandoned when a group of cubs, with their mamas, chose to make a playground out of it; they rolled over all the plants and flattened them.

However, when strangers came up to the Head in search of Jim—a game or fish warden or a hunting or fishing party—

the big bears faded from sight. Even though the visitors left in a few hours, the bears might not reappear in their customary grounds for several days.

The flats were, as well as bear-feeding grounds, a breeding place for geese and ducks. The grizzly cubs had a favorite game of peeking at the geese, then galloping at them for the sheer pleasure of seeing the birds take off in sudden, squawking flight.

The sow grizzlies paid no attention to this nonsense. However, when a cub teased its mother, she would haul off and swat it. The little imp would roll end over end across the field, then get up, with a surprised and hurt expression on its comical face, and begin to bawl.

Jim and Laurette got to recognize one gentle, half-blind old sow bear who came out each year at the Head with her current cubs. She had a face so gentle, according to Jim, that "you wanted to go up and rub her ears." She was, however, a stern disciplinarian, and expected good deportment from her various offspring. If they annoyed her, they were given a healthy swat.

Jim learned many things for himself that disproved or confirmed the tales he had heard since his childhood. Grizzlies stand erect when they are curious and want a better look. When you come upon a bear, and he rises up and peers at you, he's curious, not angry. On the other hand, when a grizzly, at the moment he sees you, comes running on all fours, he's dangerous. Out of fifty charging bears, Jim estimated that forty to forty-five are simply excited and trying to get out of the way. Six or seven are actually charging you. When they carry their heads down, and their roach rises, they mean business—dirty business.

It is useless to run from a grizzly. Despite his ponderous size, he can move at a phenomenal speed, covering fifteen to twenty feet with each leap. Actually, he walks faster than a man can run, gliding so smoothly that, at a distance, he gives the illusion of rolling along on wheels.

"If you run," Jim later advised his hunters, "run toward him—in the hope of scaring him off." But it takes a great deal of courage to run toward an attacking bear.

For years it has been held, both popularly and scientifically, that though a young grizzly cub may climb a tree, an adult grizzly either cannot or doesn't.

Jim heard on reliable authority that a sow grizzly in the interior had climbed a tree high enough to lacerate the feet of a man who was trying to escape from her. However, he had his doubts until one of his local bears did some climbing.

When Dennis's pigs were small, Jim patrolled the woods each evening for wolves. One evening he set a bait in the hope of attracting the wolves when they came for the pigs. He filled a deer's hide with entrails and put it high in a tree. When he came out the next day, it had been taken. On the trunk of the tree were the claw marks of a six- or seven-year-old grizzly. The bear had climbed up; where the trunk narrowed, he had bit off the tree until it went over, then collected the bait and run off. The diameter at the stump was only ten to twelve inches—pretty slim to support a full-grown grizzly. He had got up to where it was six inches in diameter, and obviously not strong enough to support him, then started chewing the tree down. The tracks around the tree were grizzly tracks, measuring eight inches—too large for a cub.

To those who doubt this story, Jim offers substantial proof that it was a grizzly, not a black bear, that stole the bait. First, there was a wide trail through the grass to the tree such as that made by a grizzly. Second, the black bear climbs like a telephone lineman, hugging the tree and pulling himself up, whereas the grizzly uses his long claws like a cat. Finally, the claw marks were grizzly in size—nearly twice those of a black bear.

On the basis of these episodes, Jim advises that, when chased by a grizzly, the best thing to do is to get up a tree, if one is handy—and then pray the bear hasn't learned to climb!

Two other bears were recognizable personalities; Laurette called them the Two Brothers. The first time Jim saw these young male bears, they were two-year-old cubs. As the other bears came out on the flats to dig roots and feed, the Two Brothers wrestled in mock battles. Despite the many lithographs which depict grizzlies standing erect and "boxing" with one another, the grizzly actually fights like a cat, using his claws and jaws to scratch and bite. His blows are lightning fast and, according to Jim, when one bear hits the other, it is done so fast one cannot see the movement of the paw. Contrary to popular lore, grizzlies do not "hug" their opponents, either, although one may reach out a paw and draw the other bear close enough for a good bite.

From his lookout tree, Jim watched the Two Brothers. First one would be down. Then he would wriggle out like a clever wrestler, get on his feet, swat the other one a fierce blow, and jump on him. It looked—and sounded—as though the bears were tearing each other to pieces. Yet when they paused for breath, and Jim was able to study them closely with his binoculars, there was not a mark on either one! Once he climbed down from his tree and walked up to within eighty feet of the fighting bears. They paused long enough to glance at him, then went back to their sport.

Next summer they were back, as three-year-olds, and up to the same tricks. For six summers Jim watched the Two Brothers as they grew into huge, sleek dark-brown bears. And on neither, as far as he could see, was there a scratch mark or a broken bone. The seventh year, Jim watched for them again, but they did not come out of the forest. Perhaps one of the bears was dead, and Jim did not recognize the other bear without his brother.

The old boars—grizzlies live from twenty to forty years—fought in earnest. A new bear, coming into the group, just as a new deer attempting to join a herd, might be challenged to battle. Late at night Jim and Laurette would hear their mighty roars echoing from the spruce timber.

In general, grizzlies are curious and apt to avoid, rather than provoke, trouble. Unlike the big cats who needlessly kill a herd of sheep and walk off, the grizzlies kill, not for the joy of killing, but for food. Moreover, contrary to the generally held theory that the big bears travel singly in lonely isolation, Jim found that the grizzlies were gregarious; they fed in groups around the cabin. However, if one big, powerful boar made his regal way into the area, the other would "make room" for him and scatter. Though the young bears and cubs showed due respect for the old boars, Jim never saw a boar kill a cub. On the other hand, the grizzly will attack, kill, and eat any black bear that crosses his path. Never does the grizzly show any interest in eating man. His attacks upon man are usually made in excitement, in protecting cubs, or in defending himself.

Though the Stantons were on good terms with their bear neighbors, they were always on guard. Jim kept his loaded 30-30 carbine hanging on the door, ready for trouble; but in the six years that they lived at the Head, with thirty to forty grizzlies within a few miles of their house, Jim was forced by necessity to kill only three.

11

"This Little Pig"

Though Dennis had been hairless when she first came to Kwalate, the British Columbia winters had developed a coat of hair. Bill—an eight-foot-long, pure white, bacon-type Yorkshire—had tusks. Their progeny also had hair and tusks. The little pigs inherited much of their mother's amazing personality. The summer they were old enough to scamper around and play, they discovered the cat hole in the cabin which Laurette had made so that her tomcats could get in and out at night. With a little squeezing, the piglets could inch their fat little bodies through the cat hole, too.

With the first early morning dawn, four o'clock in the summer on the Inlet, Laurette and Jim would be roused from their sleep by a scurrying, squealing parade, and ten little white pigs would come tumbling through the cat hole. When they got inside, they would grab up any loose socks or underwear they could find, run in a mad circle, reverse, and race equally madly in the opposite direction. Then, just as suddenly as they had appeared, they would drop their playthings and scramble through the cat hole, back outdoors.

White and clean, the porkers went swimming each day in the slew. They would first line up along the bank; then the older ones would take a running jump and dive in. They would disappear until halfway across, come up once for breath, and go down again. The little fellows, standing on the bank, would watch and wait and, finally getting up their courage, dive in after their elders, squealing and knotting their tails as they hit the cold water.

When the Stantons had company at the cabin, Dennis loved to come in and join them. Long after dark, when all her brood was asleep, she would slip up to the door to listen. One evening Jim, on to this trick, suddenly pulled the door open, and there was Dennis, with her ear to the door. As her support gave away, she tumbled into the room.

"Dennis, go to bed," Jim ordered sternly.

Dennis grumbled and walked off down the trail.

Ten minutes later Jim suddenly threw open the door—and again Dennis fell in.

"Oh, all right, Dennis, come on in and listen."

At this, Dennis walked in, lay down on the rug, and appeared to listen to the conversation. The Stantons swear that not once did she go to sleep when there was an opportunity to listen.

Dennis produced two litters each year, one in the spring and another in late fall. Each time she had ten white-haired, tusked pigs, all healthy and intelligent. A professional pig man, who came into the Inlet on a hunting party, declared that they were a wonderful strain which should be developed.

The Stantons had no practical use for the pigs, since Laurette refused to eat her pets, but they were proud of them and vehemently asserted that no one had pigs like Dennis and her brood.

The natural depredators of the growing drove of pigs— which eventually numbered forty—were timber wolves. From his tree, Jim regularly scouted the countryside for them, and

Dennis, too, kept careful watch. She trained her brood so well that, at any evidence of danger, she just gave them a quick command and they would "freeze" like quail. They maintained that motionless pose until she sounded the all clear.

When her pigs grew to good size, Dennis taught them to run the wolves. Jim, from his tree, watched the drama. As the wolf sneaked up on the feeding pigs, they would calmly keep on eating, until he was within thirty feet or so. Then the pigs would suddenly charge, en masse, and run the wolf back to the woods.

Though the wolves were after the pigs at every opportunity, one of the most remarkable phenomena at the Head was the relation of the bears and pigs. The pigs and the bears fed side by side in the same feeding grounds without trouble. This amicable relationship, according to Jim, may have been due to the fact that the boar grizzly and the boar pig smell almost identical; and, too, though Jim thinks the grizzly's eyesight is better than is generally believed, nevertheless it is not as keen as his ability to smell. However, if a grizzly ever tasted a dead pig, the truce was off. Like the Chinaman who burned down his house to get a pork dinner, the grizzly, from that time on, was a confirmed pig-lover. And the only choice Jim had was to get rid of the grizzly before the other bears discovered the secret.

One evening, as Jim and Laurette had just sat down to dinner, they heard a pig squeal about a quarter of a mile away. Jim grabbed his gun, shoved a box of shells into his back pocket, and ran out in the direction of the noise. Seventy-five yards from the house, he could see a two-year-old grizzly cub straddling a young pig. The mother grizzly was dancing around the scene, egging the cub on, teaching him to kill.

Jim kept firing, deliberately overshooting to miss the pig. Finally the cub rolled end over end into the grass. The sow grizzly turned and charged Jim. He pulled the trigger again. There was a click; the gun was empty. He reached into his back pocket for fresh shells and, in his haste, spilled the box onto the ground. Kneeling, his eye on the charging bear, he groped for a shell, but the grizzly was already upon him. He lifted his gun to use as a club when, just at that second, the injured pig, having got to its feet, raced between Jim and the grizzly. Her huge paw raised to swipe at Jim, the grizzly shifted aim as her eye lit on the pig, and she struck at it instead. Missing the pig, she ran after it for fifty or sixty feet, then turned back and charged Jim again. By that time Jim had found one shell and rammed it into his gun. He fired, aiming just below the ear. The one shot—which was all he had—killed her.

Hurriedly, Jim caught up with the wounded pig, a young pregnant sow, and found that she had wounds from the bear's claws in her face and shoulders. He took her home to Laurette, who put coal tar in the wounds. The pig lived, and three weeks later gave birth to eleven baby pigs!

A year later the "uneasy peace" between grizzly and pig went off balance again. One morning Jim had gone seal hunting and Laurette was alone, when she heard a pig squeal. Grabbing a coal-oil tin, she raced outside. A boar grizzly had climbed on the back of one of the pigs. Laurette grabbed a stick, beat on her oil can, and ran round and round the bear, trying to frighten him off. The noise finally drove the bear away, and he disappeared into the woods. The injured pig ran off before Laurette could get to him. That night after Jim had returned, they heard a pig squeal again, and he snatched his rifle and dashed out.

The injured pig had crawled into a salmonberry tangle and the bear had come back after him. Jim looked around uneasily. It was dark but the screams of the tortured pig drove him on. On his hands and knees, he crawled into the tangle until he could make out the dim outline of the grizzly astraddle the pig. Jim pointed his rifle barrel up to the sky, got a sight along the barrel, then carefully brought the gun down to a level with the grizzly's head and fired three times. The three shots, at fifteen feet, were true, and the grizzly, blood spurting, lunged out of the thicket, running over Jim, his breath fanning Jim's face. Forty feet from the thicket, he piled up on the ground, apparently dead. Jim made sure he was, then crawled back into the thicket and ended the pig's misery with one shot.

Laurette, waiting at the cabin, cried out in horror as Jim approached. She had heard five shots: the three that went into the bear, a fourth fired wildly as the bear ran over Jim, knocking his gun aside, and the fifth shot that killed the pig. And now she saw Jim stumbling toward the door, dripping with blood.

"You're hurt!" she cried

"No," Jim said weakly, "just done in. That's bear blood."

Laurette helped him into the house and to a chair. When he tried to roll a cigarette, the paper and tobacco shook out onto the floor. She rolled one, put it between his lips, and lit it for him.

Jim pulled gratefully on the cigarette, sat back against the chair, and some of the trembling went out of him.

"A grizzly—at fifteen feet—in the dark," he sighed. "I thought for sure I was done for. But I couldn't stand that pig's squealing in agony."

"I know," Laurette said. "Neither could I."

Oddly enough, Jim's first hunting injury had nothing to do with grizzlies. One day in midwinter, 1929, he set out to get a deer, but it was late afternoon before he got one—a fat buck. The snowfall in the forest measured eight feet, and it was impossible to pack the deer on his shoulders. The best he could do was to drag the carcass behind him.

In such weather, with a heavy snow falling, Jim always placed a little stick in the end of his gun barrel to keep the snow out, removing it, of course, before taking a shot. With darkness setting in, but only ten minutes' walk from home, Jim was moving along, carrying the plugged gun in one hand and dragging the buck's carcass with the other. As he crossed a snow bridge, it gave away and he fell through.

As he fell, he dropped his gun, butt down, and the little wood plug entered his left eye, piercing the eye muscle to the bone. The blow knocked him out and he didn't regain consciousness for two hours. When he came to, he felt the sting in his eye, thought groggily that someone had shot him, and grabbed at his gun to fire back. Then his mind cleared, and he remembered the bridge giving way, and the fall. He felt of his face in the darkness and his hand came away covered with blood. The clothes he wore were frozen fast to the ground. Carefully he pulled himself free, and crawled on hands and knees in the direction of the cabin. When he got to the door, he called, so that Laurette would know he was alive.

"Jim! Jim!" her voice shook with long-nurtured fear. "Are you all right?"

"I'm alive," he mumbled. "But don't look at me when I come in."

He pushed the door open with his foot and crawled backward into the cabin. Laurette took a deep swallow, pictured the most fearful sight she could imagine, steeled her nerves, then turned him around. Staring at his swollen, blood-streaked face, she moaned.

In a few minutes she had him in bed, his frosty clothes removed, body and face gently cleaned. The eye, where the stick had wedged in, was a livid, swollen mass. There was no thought of getting a doctor as they were frozen in for the winter. All she could do was to put on cold packs to reduce the throbbing pain.

For two weeks Jim lay in bed in the darkened cabin, his eyes covered with packs. He was too ill to stand. In addition to caring for him, Laurette had to saw wood, pack water from the spring, and feed their forty pigs.

"For once, it doesn't really seem worth it," she confessed to Jim. "I love Dennis, and I think they're all cute. But right now I wish I didn't have to worry about them and could devote all of my attention to you."

Finally, the swelling went down and Jim felt strong enough to get out of bed. But it was another two weeks before he could see light out of the injured left eye. The stick had made a bruise on the bone between the back of the eye and the brain, and eventually a cataract formed.

"But," as Jim remarked, "it wasn't my shootin' eye!"

That spring, long after his eye accident, Jim killed a seal to feed the pigs, gave each one all it should eat, then put the remainder of the meat eight feet up in a tree so that none of the pigs would glut themselves. Unfortunately, Dennis's appetite got the best of her. One night she climbed the tree, ate all the rest of the meat, and the next day died of acute indigestion—an unlikely death for such a fastidious pig.

Dennis's death took all the fun out of raising pigs. While they had often thought of selling off some of them, pig prices had been so low that it hardly seemed worth while.

Now, however, after the laborious and worrisome winter caring for her seriously injured husband and the pigs, Laurette admitted that life would be easier if they disposed of their drove. Besides, the money they received for the porkers—however little it was—would be welcome. Although the Stantons were somewhat better off than in the early Kwalate days, they still didn't have enough money to feel secure. If they did get some cash put aside, there was sure to be a severe winter, and Laurette would—warmly and willingly—feed strangers and Indians until spring. That left them broke again.

So they located a market in Alert Bay, and made a deal to deliver their pigs for 2½ cents a pound on the hoof. Laurette insisted upon an understanding that the pigs were not to be used for meat, but for breeding only. If any were killed, for any reason, she stipulated that they must be shot with a rifle.

It was a twenty-four-hours round trip to Alert Bay. The pigs were so big and healthy that the boat could hold only two of them at a time; they were so tame that they jumped in the boat, on order, and at Alert Bay followed Laurette off the boat, at her heels, like dogs. She was heart broken to "lead them to slaughter," as she put it, and Jim still recalls the sight of Laurette, marching up the main street, her head high and tears running down her face, with two fat, happy pigs heeling, in line behind her.

"If I ever hear of one of those pigs being butchered," Laurette firmly declared, "I'll just butcher that man!"

"If he knew you as I do," Jim grinned, "he wouldn't dare take the chance."

12

Lord of the Woods

Every year, on April 17, the Mussel Creek grizzly came
down the mountain from his winter bed around Mussel Creek
to feed on the flats. An outsized boar, this four-legged giant
came out on exactly the same date for the eight years the
Stantons lived at the head of the Inlet; and Jim encountered
him, in early winter on his trap line, for another twelve years.
A mighty old warrior who feared no comers, he could be
heard fifteen minutes before he actually appeared.

His fearless actions seemed to be due to the sense of security
which his size and age inspired, for a huge, lumbering grizzly
can be either noisy or silent. If he is panicked and running
wildly, he can be heard crashing through the forest for as
much as a mile away. But if he is sneaking up on something,
he can, despite his size, move through the brush without so
much as a rustle of leaves.

When hunted, a big bear will often bounce out of sight into
a dense patch of brush. Then there is complete silence. But
when the hunter "makes the big sneak" and creeps in to the
spot where he believes the bear to be, there is nothing there.
The animal has slipped off without crackling a twig. While a
young buck deer will sail through the woods, depending on
his superior speed to carry him from danger, the old buck,

just as the old grizzly, will crouch down under cover of the brush and sneak silently away.

The Mussel Creek grizzly's noise was both authority and warning. At the sound of his approach, the other grizzlies, feeding on the flats, would listen—then fade off to the sides of the field, leaving the main feeding ground for the old boar. He was a "goer-alone," this giant that no other grizzly dared to antagonize.

Though the grizzlies frequently fed in groups in the field, each adult had a separate "fishing preserve"—a certain territory which he considered his private property, running off any other bear who tried to get on it. One adult bear's territory would run nearly a mile along a fishing creek; then, a quarter of a mile beyond, another's would begin. Though some of the young bears argued their boundaries, none seemed to care to challenge the Mussel Creek grizzly, who had the longest foot tracks of any bear in the area—a full fourteen inches.

While he was wary the first few months, the Mussel Creek grizzly soon decided the Stantons were "safe." When he roared out of his winter bed in April, his objective, in addition to wild rhubarb roots, was the fish heads which Laurette put out for him. He would stand in the woodshed, beside the little cabin—which he could easily have pushed over by leaning on—eat his fish heads, then wander out in the field to graze.

On the trap line, in early winter, when he came along the bear's territory and met him on the trail, Jim would stop, roll a cigarette, and wait. The big grizzly, seeing him standing there, would move aside, off the trail, and let him go by. Yet when any other person came into the area, the big bear disappeared until he had gone.

By now, Jim's reputation as an expert on grizzly hunting

brought him much business as a guide. Since the Mussel Creek grizzly was the finest trophy bear in the territory, and an old boar who was no longer keeping up the herd, Jim decided to take one of the big-game hunters in to get him. The man was a wealthy banker who had come to get "the biggest trophy bear he could find."

Jim led his hunter, armed with a "real cannon" of a gun, into the woods to the tunnel which led to the big grizzly's day bed. They stayed there a while, waiting for the old fellow to come out for his daily fishing, but the banker soon got tired of waiting.

"Can't you scare him out for me, Jim?" he asked. "I don't want to stand around here all day."

Jim put the banker on a stand in front of the tunnel, then, sneaking up behind, came down on the bear's bed. As Jim crept close, he could hear the big fellow's sonorous breathing. He got up to a windfall log where the breathing was loudest, peeked over, and there lay the Mussel Creek grizzly, sound asleep. The wind had died, and the old bear didn't get the scent and waken. Jim watched the snoring giant for a moment, then said, "Woof!" The bear reared up, roared, and headed out of the tunnel.

Jim started back, waiting for the hunter's shot. There was silence. He hurried around, found his banker still on the stand where he had left him, the "cannon" cocked and ready in his hand, his face blanched with fear. The old grizzly was long gone, but Jim could hear him crashing through the forest with great twenty-foot leaps.

"Why didn't you shoot?" Jim asked.

"My God, I didn't know he was so big!" the banker gasped. "I was scared to shoot, and thought I'd wait till he got by. But then he moved so fast, he was out of range before I got my aim——"

"Yeah, he can move when he takes a notion," Jim said, smiling, pleased in spite of himself that the big bear had got away.

The banker put down his "cannon" and laid his hand on Jim's arm. "Take me out of here," he said quietly. "I'm no bear hunter."

"All right," Jim agreed. "Maybe we'd better go fishing."

"That," the hunter said, "will suit me just fine."

A few years later Jim's amicable relationship with the Mussel Creek grizzly was interrupted for a time by an accident which was nearly fatal. A young German boy who had come up to the Inlet was in need of money, and Jim agreed to take him out on his trap line and let him share the profits in exchange for his help and companionship. The muscular nineteen-year-old had bragged about what an athlete he was and how easily he could swim two miles; but one mile of trail, trying to keep up with Jim's dogtrot, got him down. It was a long hike to the Mussel Lake cabin, and Jim always hurried to make sure he got in before dark. The boy kept sitting down to ease his cramped legs, and the only way Jim could get him to move was to go off and leave him.

The trail led along the creek which branched inland from Klinaklini, and ten or twelve bears fished along it, among them the Mussel Creek grizzly. The giant bear had made his bed right on Jim's trail, and it had lately been Jim's practice, as he neared the spot, to rattle the machete he always carried against the barrel of his 30-30 rifle. At this warning sound, the bear would waken, get up from his bed, and stand off the trail till Jim went by. But this time, in his effort to hurry the boy, Jim forgot about the bear, and failed to give him the warning sound.

It was nearly dusk as Jim hustled along the mossy piece

of trail near the bear's bed, the sound of his steps muffled by the soft moss; the German boy, rifle in hand, trailed behind him. They got within twenty feet of the bear's bed before the grizzly heard them and woke from his sleep. The old warrior rose—and charged.

Within a matter of three jumps he would be on top of them. Jim yelled, threw his machete at the bear, and fired without putting his gun to his shoulder. The shot went through the grizzly's lungs, but the bear kept on coming—until his huge body was against the barrel of Jim's gun. Jim shot again—and the shell failed to explode. The grizzly pushed Jim back against the German boy, then rushed on by. Jim shoved another shell into his gun, firing at the grizzly's back. The bear crashed into a grove of fir trees and disappeared. It was almost dark, and because Jim felt sure the lung shot would prove fatal in a matter of minutes, he did not follow the grizzly into the dense brush.

Next morning Jim went back to the place where he had shot his old friend. He crawled into the thicket were the bear had disappeared and found blood—but no bear. There was more blood ten or fifteen feet beyond. Jim took up this trail and followed it to a rocky hill where it suddenly disappeared. There was no more blood, and no tracks. He hunted all day long and finally was forced to give up.

Four weeks later Jim found the Mussel Creek grizzly back on his bed. Once more Jim rattled his machete on his gun barrel; once more the giant rose from his bed and stepped out of the way until Jim passed. He seemed to hold no grudge, nor did he connect the shooting with Jim. Jim saw the bear for another four years—until he finally disappeared, dying, probably, from plain old age.

The fact that the lung shot had not been fatal worried Jim. It was scarcely reassuring to a man who was in daily contact with bears. When he had to shoot, Jim wanted his shots to count. He liked his old 30-30—but it obviously was not big enough for a really tough rascal like the Mussel Creek grizzly. Jim put in an order for a new, more powerful rifle, a 348 Winchester.

In spite of his experience with the Mussel Creek grizzly, Jim insists that the grizzly shows definite reasoning power and shrewdness, and he rates its intelligence over that of a dog or a horse. He tells the story of how the grizzly escaped his historic enemy the Indian and his cunning deadfall traps.

To make certain there was no scent on the traps, the Indians made them in the spring and left them propped open all summer along an animal trail until the human scent disappeared and the animals became accustomed to the trap and walked through it. Then in the fall the Indians would take the prop away and set the trap so that when a grizzly walked into it, half a ton of rocks or a half-dozen giant logs would drop down and kill him. This method worked on a few grizzlies, but the following generation learned to recognize the deadfall traps by *sight,* rather than scent, and eventually all grizzlies walked around them.

From the vantage point of his 150-foot spruce tree. Jim has observed just how cagey the big bears can be. Once, when he was expecting a party by boat, Jim saw a grizzly digging roots out in the open field. When the bear heard the distant rumble of the motor, he stopped eating, ran 150 yards to a bush, got down behind it, then peeked around and watched the boat coming up the slew. He didn't "take to the woods," but instinctive caution kept him from being an open target.

Jim has a healthy respect for the grizzly's strength and the damage he can do. "He's got a wheel on each corner, a mind of his own, and he goes where he wants to," Jim says.

In all their years around the bears, which included the raising of three pets, neither Jim nor Laurette ever actually touched a grizzly—though they were often tempted.

Once when Laurette was out on the slew bank, she saw a mother bear and two tiny puffball cubs that she itched to lay hands on. She crept up until she was within ten feet of the mother, and barely an arm's length from the nearest cub. Just as she reached her arm out to touch the little round fellow, who was looking at her with curious, unafraid eyes, Laurette felt herself being roughly yanked away—by the seat of her slacks.

"Don't ever try that again!" Jim said fiercely. He had come around the side of the house in time to snatch her. "We've got along pretty well in these woods by keeping hands off. Just touch that cub—and figure what the old sow would do to you!"

Laurette admitted she had been wrong. It was a temptation to take hold of wild things, but safety lay in restraining the impulse. Any time a grizzly got too familiar, or became curious about the inside of their cabin, they were in for trouble.

Jim was very careful not to leave food with an odor around his cabins, so the bears didn't learn of either man or man's food. And the bears' natural food was so plentiful they were not ravenous enough to trail a faint scent. In the interior, however, with many trappers and many cabins, and some careless cooks who left the remains of food about, the bears had made the association, and trappers had constant trouble with bears' raiding and destroying their trapping cabins. If they barricaded the doors and put sharp saws across, the grizzly would go around, trying all the doors and windows. If he couldn't get in that way, he would go up on the roof and claw the shakes off until he had a hole large enough to drop down inside. The only protection was to cache supplies on a platform in a tall tree, remove the ladder, and open the door of the cabin. The grizzly would walk in the door, look around, and after inspecting what was inside and seeing no food, he would then go away quite peacefully.

One huge bear—next to the Mussel Creek grizzly the biggest one on the flats—came around each summer and, it seemed to Jim, became increasingly interested in the Stanton cabin. He learned where they placed their gill net in the slew, and he would go down and wait beside the net so that he could get the fish heads when Laurette took out the salmon and cleaned them. He also appeared regularly at their woodshed and beside the back porch. Though he seemed peaceful enough, Jim became increasingly concerned. Every time he or Laurette stepped out to get a stick of firewood, they had to walk around the enormous bear. As time approached for trapping, and the big fellow hung on, Jim decided to kill him. He couldn't leave Laurette alone in the cabin with this thousand-pounder hovering around. If she accidentally got in the big fellow's way, and he put out a mammoth paw to shove her aside, it would probably be a killing blow. A single smack from a grizzly has been known to break the back of a grown steer, kill a horse, and paralyze a buck deer.

The bear had been coming around for four years, never showing anything but an equable disposition. However, the day that Jim made up his mind to kill him, and walked out of the cabin, the bear ran from him and hid behind a bush. When Jim came on, the big bear's hackles rose, and he charged.

Jim fired, the shot went true, and the bear fell. Then he rose and Jim fired again. The second time the bear lay still, but he opened his mouth in a final effort to bite. Jim came in close and finished him with a third shot. The grizzly, like any big game, is hard to kill, particularly if the hunter is at close range and allows him to rise after knocking him down.

"I wonder how he knew," Jim mused later that night. "You know, he ran from me when I walked out this morning."

"He knew death," Laurette said. "All the animals know death. And," she said, chidingly, "they know which people kill, too!"

Jim wasn't sure about their sense of death, but he had certainly learned about their sense of smell. Once when he was up in his spruce tree watching five bears eating out on the flats, they suddenly rose up, full length, and began to sniff. They stood for a moment, facing the salt water two miles away, their noses and lips wrinkling as they located—and defined—the scent; then all five turned as one and tore off for the woods. Fifteen minutes later a strange boat passed the point. The bears had smelled the strange human scent two miles away.

Like the deer, the grizzlies, when they get a faint scent, wet their noses with their tongues and smell again—refreshing the scent with the moisture.

Once Jim was out on the flats with a hunter, and both men were wearing hip-length rubber boots, which are supposed to leave no scent. The next day—thirty hours later, after the noon sun had beaten down on their boot tracks—Jim saw a bald-faced grizzly get the scent from the tracks, clamber on a snag and look around, go back and sniff the scent again, and high-tail it for the woods.

In the glacial and mountain areas, particularly where they had no human contact, human scent alone often frightened the bears. More than once Jim sailed his hat into the face of a charging grizzly, and the human scent of the hat sent the bear lumbering off into the brush.

In the late 1920's mountain climbers developed an active interest in the series of peaks rimming the upper head of Knight Inlet. It was sparked by a well-known mountain climber and naturalist, Don Munday, and his wife, of Vancouver. They wanted to scale the tallest peak in the region—then called the Unknown Mountain and later named by Munday Mount Waddington, for an early explorer of British Columbia. The peaks in the region were particularly difficult because of large glacial fields which lay around their bases. The Franklin Glacier, with an ice field of 110 square miles, and the Klinaklini Glacier, with 325 square miles, made going hazardous.

Jim packed the Mundays in over the Franklin Glacier for several unsuccessful attempts at scaling Mount Waddington; he also packed in the Fritz Weissner party which conquered it.

When they were exploring and climbing, the Mundays often left their young daughter, Edith, with Jim and Laurette, and she developed a completely fearless attitude toward grizzlies. The summer that she was eleven, one big grizzly got into the habit of staying close around their cabin where she played. Jim tried to drive the bear off but it wouldn't go. Not wishing to kill him, Jim got his 22 rifle and shot the bear in the backside, just nicking him. The grizzly felt the prick of the bullet, looked reproachfully at Jim, and then, with a completely ludicrous gesture, reached around and scratched where the bullet had hit. Jim exchanged the 22 rifle for a shotgun, and fired a loud blast over the bear's head. The grizzly gazed at Jim again in annoyance, and then went back to eating.

This was not the first time Jim had found that individual bears differ widely in their reactions. When he wanted to get rid of a bear, he could sometimes scare him off with a harsh yell or by merely waving his hat. The biggest of bears might lunge off into the woods at the slightest sound or gesture. Again, one might stand his ground, giving Jim a "dirty look," his hackles beginning to rise. "Then," says Jim, "watch out!"

13

The Big Freeze

Their fourth winter at the Head, the ground was frozen solid from early fall. Just at Christmas, a royal chinook—a south wind—blew in, creating a midwinter thaw. Taking advantage of it, Laurette and Jim high-tailed it to Minstrel Island and replenished their provisions. The proprietor of the hotel and his wife, who were old friends, wanted them to stay over for New Year's dinner.

"No—we'd better get on," Jim said, with a glance at the sky. "Don't know how long this chinook will hold. We've got to get back in with it, or we'll never get in."

With a sigh of regret for the tempting turkey dinner, Jim and Laurette loaded the supplies on their gas-boat and waved good-by. They covered thirty miles of the return trip and reached Glendale Cove, halfway to their home, where they stopped for the night, then started early again the next morning. Sailing out from Glendale in a mild southeast wind, they had barely reached the middle of the Inlet when the wind suddenly shifted to northwest.

"Look what's coming!" Laurette cried.

A few miles down the Inlet they could see a white squall, a veritable wall of water roaring up the Inlet toward them.

"I can't get back to Glendale now," Jim said soberly. "We'll have to ride it out where we are."

Within five minutes they could not see the shore, scarcely a hundred yards away. Then, at their side, they made out another boat which seemed to be helplessly running in to shore.

"I'll try to give him a hand," Jim yelled over the roar of the wind.

As he made a turn to throw a line to the other boat and pull it off the rocks, the sea broke over him, drenching him, and filling the afterhold. Laurette grabbed a bucket and began to bail. As Jim fought for control of the boat, the wind carried it into the lee shore. They could hear the scraping of rocks beneath them as they rounded the point on the lee beach.

The man whom Jim had tried to help— "You don't pass up anyone in trouble in this country"—had got his anchor down and was holding his boat off the rocks with a pole.

Though their boat had ceased to fill, Jim found he couldn't control it in the savage northwest wind. As the wild gusts caught it, the little boat skated like a chip of wood along the water. There was nothing to do but hang on and pray.

Finally, in late afternoon they reached their home slew at the Head—jolted, terrified, but still alive. They pulled the boat up, unloaded the supplies, and hurried to the cabin. By dark the slew was already freezing and by morning there were seven inches of ice—not a chance of getting in or out until the spring thaw.

With the big freeze on, the cabin suddenly became a relief station. The man whose boat they had seen running up the Inlet turned out to be a friend named Stewart, who had come in for a three-day duck hunt. He reached the Head, but was forced to stay until the spring thaw. Fortunately he could sleep on his boat, but for the next three months he took his meals with Laurette and Jim.

Three Indian families who had come up in the fall to trap—

intending to get out by New Year's—were also caught in the freeze. They had their cabins on the river, but they had only enough food to last until January. There were men, women, and children, and one five-month-old baby. The day after the freeze, they appeared at the cabin, explaining their plight.

Laurette went through her supplies, got out flour, potatoes, sugar, tea, beans, and rice, which, added to deer meat the men could shoot, might carry them through. Then she reached into her precious store of canned milk to get out enough to feed the baby.

"After our first winter at Kwalate," she explained, "I learned to keep enough supplies for at least four people besides ourselves. In country like this, you must feed anyone who comes around. If you don't, they may starve."

In March, when the first spring thaw came, Stewart hurriedly left for home, and the Indians clambered into their boat and disappeared down the Inlet. In a few days they were back. Instead of returning to their homes on the coast, they had gone to the store at Minstrel Island, bought supplies, and come back up the Head to repay Laurette.

"We got lots of food now," they told her, "flours, potatoes —you take food."

Laurette refused, smiling. "You keep your food," she said; "then some day, we will be hungry, and we will come to you."

This idea seemed to pleased the little group, and, thanking Laurette again, they got in their boats and sped down the Inlet. As they left, they waved good-by saying, "We see you at oolichan time!"

"Oolichan time" came in the spring during the oolichan run, and was an important time for the Indians. They not only dried the rich, oily fish for food, but extracted the oil which they used for cooking and as a health remedy. The Indians have used this natural medicine for centuries, and their methods of manufacturing it have never changed. They leave the fish in vats until it rots, put it in cookers and add water; then as the oil comes to the top, they skim it off and put it up in five-gallon tins.

The bins of maggot-infested rotting fish scarcely seemed a promise of health, but the oolichan oil was a source of vitamins for the Indians, particularly during the winter months when their diet was limited to dried meat and fish and bread. In the influenza epidemic of 1918, the Indians who regularly took the oil had survived, but those who did not, had succumbed to the disease.

The offensive odor from the vats of rotten fish was to the Indians a token of the power of their medicine. "Indians like plenty of smell," Chief Tom Duncan explained to Jim. *Hyui skookum hummm*—very strong smell—was a phrase of praise rather than condemnation. And *hummm* grease—stinking oil —was their name for this popular medicine.

Once when Charlie Panqwit came to call, Laurette offered him some of her precious Camembert cheese, the single luxury she permitted herself when ordering winter provisions each fall. He refused it, holding his nose to show his reason. A few days later Laurette went to the Indian camp and found Charlie working in the oolichan vats. She held her nose, saying, *"Hyui skookum!"*

Charlie nodded. "Just like white man's cheese!" he said.

When the Indian boats reappeared on the Inlet, they all made a "first stop" at the Stantons'. For Laurette there was potlatch—a little gift from each family: home-canned clams, store-bought glass dishes, choice pieces of fresh halibut. After that winter, from a sort of neutral amicability, the Stantons' relationship with their Indian neighbors changed to a more personal one, and they soon became good friends with many of them.

Sarah, Tom's wife, furnished the brains and business sense for the tribe. Since she knew English and could figure, she handled all dealings with the Indian agent, the fur buyers, and storekeepers. Her own three children had died of tuberculosis and she had adopted a boy whom she named William. He was her only adopted child, but each season Sarah took a new, temporary crop of children whom she hoped to aid and influence through her own excellent educational background and warm heart.

In the years that followed, Laurette and Sarah became fast friends. They had many things in common besides warmth and vitality. For one thing, they were both musicians. Every few nights, when they were at the Inlet, the Indian families gathered at the Stantons' for a "sing song," and Laurette and Sarah spelled each other at the piano. Years later, when Sarah's first granddaughter, William's child, was born, she was christened Laurette.

Tom Duncan's brother was named Bob Harris. The different surnames resulted from a commercial transaction. The brothers had "bought" different names. The Scottish trappers who came up into the Inlet country had shown their habitual shrewdness by selling their names to the Indians in exchange for valuable furs. A long name, like Dinwiddie, sold for ten dollars' worth of furs, but a short name, like Duncan or Harris, brought only five.

Between the Scotsmen, who were often squawmen during the trapping season, and the Kanakas—South Seas sailors who jumped ship along the coast—the coastal Indians were an heterogeneous mixture, which showed up in their varied coloring, attitudes, and manners.

One of the Stantons' most interesting neighbors was a white

woodsman, Forest Johnson. Forest's father had come, along with his strapping sons, from the Kentucky woods to the wilds of British Columbia when Forest was a boy, and settled in the region of Jarvis Inlet. Forest had grown up in the woods, trapping and logging, and living among the Indians. Nearly six feet four, with a muscular, lean body and handsome, strong-featured face, Forest was, it seemed to Jim, the epitome of the traditional frontiersman of the woods. Even in the coldest winter he wore no more than a rough shirt, pants, shoes and socks. He glided through the forest at a tireless trot, knew every animal, bird, insect, and plant that lived in the woods. Though uneducated, he had a marvelous memory; his Indian wife, who had been to school and learned to read and write, took care of whatever business affairs they had.

Out in the woods with Jim, Forest would suddenly stop for no apparent reason, reach down and dig out a piece of root from the forest floor, or peel some bark from a tree, then hand it to Jim. It was always, Jim discovered, something edible and delicious—the old-time woodsman could literally "live on roots" if he must.

Taking whatever jobs appeared, Forest trapped, fished, hunted along the coast, and sometimes served as a guide. The story went that just before World War I, he had taken a white hunter out into the wilderness. As they climbed a mountain the hunter stumbled and fell backward, carrying Forest with him down a steep slope. The hunter suffered fractures of both legs; Forest broke two ribs and completely shattered his right elbow. Despite his own painful injuries, Forest got the hunter on his back and carried him out of the woods to a river, where he could be put on a boat and headed for a hospital. Forest refused to go along and have his own injuries tended to. He had never been to a doctor or hospital, and he had no intention of going now. Instead, he went to an Indian doctor in the tribe with which he was living. The old Indian tied off the upper arm to deaden pain and split open the elbow. He carefully set all the bone fragments in place, then bandaged it. Each day he came to see his patient and gently worked the arm. In a matter of a few months Forest was as active as ever and when the World War I began, Forest, as a good Kentuckian, volunteered in the United States Army. When he came up for his medical examination, he told about his shattered elbow. The Army doctors made an examination, tested the use he had of the arm, and pronounced it a perfect job of healing.

Jim's Indian neighbors were rivermen and canoemen, but seldom any good in the woods. Removed from water, they were apt to get into trouble. One day when he was out on his trap line, Jim came across Chief Bob Harris, a young Indian named Williams, and his sixteen-year-old wife lost in the woods. They had been on their trapping grounds, eighteen miles upriver from home, when their canoe got away from them. Cutting over the hills in an effort to find Jim's trap line and follow it out, they had got lost, and when Jim found them, they had been three days without food, and Harris was suffering from exposure and exhaustion.

Jim took them to his trapping cabin and fed them. That night Chief Bob, an asthmatic, sat down on the floor and propped his back against the wall to sleep. The other three got in the bed, the girl next to the wall, her husband next to her, and Jim on the outside.

The young Indian wife was too amused at the situation to go to sleep. Apparently the idea of being in bed with two men, one red and one white, struck her as very funny.

Next day Jim brought them out of the woods, carrying Harris, as the Chief was too ill to walk. The day after, an

Indian child brought Laurette a large fresh salmon. From then on, the Stantons regularly received gifts from Chief Bob: fresh fish, dishes, sacks of clams. The Chief, meanwhile, spread the story over the Inlet of how Jim had saved his life.

Three years later, when Jim and Laurette were in the store at Minstrel Island, a plump young woman with two small children came up and spoke to them.

Laurette, not recognizing the girl, said, "I'm sorry, I don't place you."

"Oh," she giggled, "I'm the girl who slept with your husband!"

For any Indian who appeared at the Stanton cabin, there was the assurance of tea, bread and jam, cookies for the small fry—and a friendly listening ear. Though she never again had to pull three families through a winter, Laurette kept a stock of simple medicines which she doled out as needed, and she was good for a "loan" of some staple food at any time. To Jim fell the job of settling disputes. One old Indian who had bought a thousand feet of lumber left it in Jim's charge. "If I die, it's your lumber; if I come back, it's mine." When the old man didn't show up the next season, Jim thought he must had died, but he kept the lumber intact. Three years later, the Indian appeared and happily claimed his lumber. "I no die—it's mine!"

One fall morning Charlie Panqwit appeared at the Stanton cabin, obviously distressed.

"What's wrong, Charlie?" Laurette asked.

"Wife sick," Charlie said. "She cry. She hurt here"—touching his throat—"and here"—touching his chest—"and here"—touching his belly— "You doctor, Mrs. Kwalate. You do something."

Laurette opened her medicine chest, got out aspirin, and

gave Charlie a demonstration of how to dissolve it in water and gargle.

Charlie nodded sagely. "M'mm—wash throat!"

Next Laurette got out chest plasters, the application of which he seemed to understand. Then she brought out Sal Hepatica—on the suspicion that Mrs. Panqwit's bellyache was due to a diet of pilot bread, which the Indians ate all through the trapping season.

Loaded with medicines and instructions, Charlie went on his way with the promise that he would report results.

Three days later he appeared at the cabin, smiling broadly.

"You good doctor," he told Laurette. "Wife no hurt, no cry."

One evening, later on, when Sarah Duncan was sitting quietly in front of the fire beside Jim, and Laurette was busy in the kitchen, Sarah said softly, "Not nice to talk of now, Jim. But when Laurette dies, she's going to have the finest funeral of any Indian on the coast."

14

Not a Doctor in the House

In a country teeming with wildlife of all kinds, it was still a problem for Jim to find enough bait for his traps. The Game Department, in its efforts to preserve game and fish, allowed only certain bait to be used. Legal bait had been scarce, but one morning in the fall of 1930 Jim managed to gaff out a thirty-pound spring salmon. He immediately set out for the Mussel Lake cabin, baiting his marten traps on the way so that he would have fur to take out when he came back. By the time he reached the lake, snow was falling fast, and promised to keep up steadily throughout the night, but there was still about twenty minutes of light left. Leaving his gear at the cabin, he took bait for three traps, scurried up the next day's trail, baited three traps, and got back to the cabin just as night fell.

When he rose the next morning, nearly a foot of snow had fallen. Downing his usual breakfast of flapjacks and coffee, then sealing up his food supplies, Jim hurried up the trail toward the cabin at Laurel Lake. At the first trap which he had baited the night before, he found that the bait had been taken but no animal trapped. In the soft fresh snow, leading to the trap, were the tracks of a sow grizzly and a two-year-old cub. Jim re-baited the trap, moved on—and the bear tracks led him straight to his second trap. The bait had been stolen from it, too. Old Mama grizzly was picking up his precious bait as fast as he put it down.

Jim wasn't often troubled by bears' going after his bait. Feeding conditions were good enough in the area so that they didn't hunt for tidbits of food. But the unseasonable snow had made fish scarce, and Mama and her cub were hungry.

As he waded through the fresh, wet snow, on the seven-mile trek to Laurel Lake, Jim was worried. The salmon was all he had to set his line. If Mama grizzly came along, eating it up as fast as he baited, he was out of luck for the whole trip. And if he was lucky enough to get another fish and re-bait, she'd probably get that, too. His whole season's trapping was in jeopardy. She knew where the food was now, and would keep coming back until there wasn't any more to eat.

By the time he reached the Laurel Lake cabin, Jim was soaking wet from the soft snow. He baited a marten set near the cabin; then he went in, made a fire, ate a little supper— and thought of that grizzly coming along to steal his bait.

It was now or never. If he let the grizzly win, he might as well get off the trapping line, but he couldn't afford to do that. Money was still very scarce.

Wearily, but with determination, Jim filled the little car-bide pit-light which he carried with him to use in the cabins at night, went out to the marten set, and crawled up on a rock over the set to wait. The cold, black winter night had settled in, and as he sat on the rock in his wet clothes, waiting for the two bears to come up through the darkness, Jim began to shiver—partly from cold, partly from fear. Facing two bears in pitch darkness took real courage. If he started shooting, he would have to get them both. There was scant hope of their running off after night had set in. Night was their ally, and the enemy of man.

Finally his straining ears caught the sound he was waiting for: the heavy-breathed blowing and puffing of the two grizzlies as they came along the trail sniffing for bait. Jim's numbed fingers reached for the flint on his carbide light, but he was shivering so that his fingers wouldn't function. He couldn't flip on the light with which he had hoped to pit-light the bears' eyes in order to get a good shot. The bears heard the impotent scratching of Jim's fingers on the flint— they stopped, listened, then ran.

When he heard them crashing off into the woods, Jim felt suddenly sick. He climbed off the rock, sprang the trap, and stumbled into the cabin. He managed to get a little fire going in the hearth and knelt beside it, trying to get warm. But even after the warmth had reached him, his hands were still trembling and his body was shivering convulsively. Worst of all, his jaws felt as though he had a football in his mouth, and he could hardly see out of his eyes. Uneasily, Jim ran his hands over his face and throat. It wasn't imagination. His jaws *were* swollen to twice their normal size. And the swelling extended up into his face, so that his eyes were narrowed down to slits. There was something far more wrong with him than wet and cold and fear.

He was seriously ill, and a long way from home. In each cabin was enough wood and food to sustain him for a week or ten days, but he was too sick to take care of himself. He must make it home to Laurette's care, or he would die.

At daybreak he forced down some breakfast, loaded his pack, and set out on the trail, springing his traps as he went. The way he felt, it would be a long time before he would be back on his line again.

Fighting through the snowstorm that raged around him, trying to conquer the violent pain in his jaws and head, Jim slowly made his way from Laurel to Mussel Lake. But he could go no farther that day. The snowstorm had added another foot to the previous fall.

He stumbled into the cabin and sat hunched over a fire all night long. Outside, the wind brought a new blanket of snow. He would need all his strength to fight his way through such a storm, but he had no thought of sleep. His jaws and head were aching as though someone were beating on them with a hammer.

By morning Jim's face was swollen worse than ever. He managed to pry one eye open enough to see the trail before him, and set out on the last ten miles toward home. He shivered constantly, and a great weakness coursed through his body, making progress increasingly slow and painful. He hiked for an hour, then sat down and rested for ten minutes, pulled himself up, hiked another hour, then sat down to rest again. Each time he sat down, the temptation was stronger than ever to go to sleep in the snow. The pain had given way to a numbness that conquered his whole body, and took away all motive, all reason. He wanted only to lie in the snow. However, he knew that if he did, Laurette would come after him. Jim forced his weary mind to grasp that thought and hold it, like a beacon in front of him, forcing him forward.

Just before dark that evening Jim finally saw the cabin before him—like some mirage toward which he had been endlessly journeying.

When he stumbled through the door of his house—his face distorted to the size of a balloon—Laurette was terrified.

"If we could only get a doctor!" she cried out. "You've *got* to have a doctor!"

The slew in front of the cabin was frozen solid; there wasn't a chance of getting a boat out. Laurette could only put Jim to bed, get a big fire going, put dry, warm clothes on him— and pray. There was nothing that she knew of that would reduce the swelling, which actually seemed to increase as she watched.

The next day Jim's lower jaw broke open under the pressure of infection and began discharging fluid, but the release of the poison brought him no relief. His heart pounded frighteningly; his entire body was racked with pain. The poison was seeping through his whole system.

For thirty days he lay in bed, the jaw seeping, his body growing weaker and weaker. Not a soul came near the cabin. Not a boat was heard on the Inlet. Laurette spent most of her time on the blizzard-swept beach, "bucking up" driftwood with a crosscut saw to keep the fire going.

On the thirtieth day, Jim made up his mind. He must do something or he would die. The infection was obviously coming from two of his teeth, and they must come out. He went about planning in the careful, methodical fashion in which he figured his trap lines, his hand logging, all the dangerous work in which he had engaged. Then he explained his plan to Laurette and she agreed.

"Bring in the blacksmith anvil from the woodshed," he ordered. When she had lugged in the thirty-five-pound anvil, he said, "Now get three of those empty wooden milk cases."

She stacked them on top of each other, then managed to heave the anvil on top. Next he had her get a cork line—a cotton line about the size of a finger, which stands a 2,000-pound strain, and a sixty-pound-test linen fishing line. He made a loop in the linen line and put it over one of his infected teeth, working it down close to the gum and cinching it as tight as he could. Laurette then tied it to the cork line and threaded the cork line up through a little galvanized pulley that Jim had instructed her to attach to a rafter over the bed. She played out the line down to the anvil which rested on the wood crates, cocked the anvil, off balance and ready to fall from the crates, and took the end of the line from the anvil to Jim. Jim had estimated the angle of lead—from tooth to pulley—to anvil. If his figuring was correct, the tooth would come out when he pulled the line that tipped the anvil. If his angle was estimated wrong, or if the tooth was stubborn and refused to come, the force of the jolt could break his jaw.

When all was ready, and he held the string in his hand, Jim motioned to Laurette.

"Get up here," he said, "and sit straddle of my stomach, to brace the shock. Put both your hands on my forehead, and brace with your hands and body. Then maybe we at least won't break my neck."

White-faced but firm, Laurette did as she was told. Then Jim drew up one knee and braced his elbow against it; the palm of his hand supported his chin to hold it as steady as possible.

"Ready?" he asked.

"Ready," Laurette whispered.

Jim took one long deep breath, uttered a silent prayer—and pulled the string with his free hand.

The anvil crashed to the floor and the line over the pulley jerked up the slack. The 150-pound pressure flew down the line to the tooth, and, with a tremendous pop, the tooth shot out of Jim's mouth and dangled up in the air above them.

When he could get his mouth clear of pus and blood, Jim squealed weakly, "Something sure came out, all right!"

Laurette's eyes were bright with relief. "Oh, Jim, you really figured that right!"

"Guess I did," he agreed. "Now we might as well get the other one while we're at it."

Once more Laurette set the props—a line around Jim's other infected tooth, to the cork line, through the pulley, to the anvil, to Jim's hand. Once more she climbed astraddle, braced his body for the shock, and he pulled the string. The other tooth bounced out, swinging neatly over them.

Almost from that moment, Jim began to feel better. The fever—which had burned unceasingly for thirty days—slackened; the swelling began to go down. He could feel his heart quieting, relieved of the strain of fighting the poison in his blood.

It had been a terrific chance to take. If any of his calculations had been off—— But he had remembered one of the old laws of weights and distance—the law of falling weight—the distance plus the weight of the anvil falling to the floor equaled approximately 150-pounds pressure, enough to uproot the most tenacious of human teeth—or yank off his whole head if he was wrong.

Four days later, when the slew began to thaw, Jim felt strong enough to head out alone in the boat to see if he could locate a dentist. His amateur dental job should be completed. At Glendale, Pat King, the new cannery watchman, took one look at Jim and volunteered to help him. An itinerant dentist was reputedly working at Minstrel Island, thirty miles away, but there they got the discouraging news that the dentist had moved on to Symoon Sound, another thirty miles away. Reaching Symoon, they were told that the dentist had just left for Greenway—twenty-five miles. Doggedly they trailed him to Greenway, then spent a day cruising around the sound before they finally located him, pulling teeth in a logging camp.

Dr. Davies looked into Jim's mouth and shook his head. "You have seven teeth that should come out, Mr. Stanton. You're in bad shape, sir. You should go straight to Vancouver and enter the hospital where the job can be done under the best conditions."

"Nope." Jim shook his head. "I'm not going to Vancouver.

I've got to get this over with and go back to the Head. My wife's alone up there with no boat and no help within thirty miles."

"It'll be a terrible job for both of us," Dr. Davies warned. "Four of those teeth are wisdom teeth."

"I'll help," offered Mrs. Mann, the logger's wife.

Jim took his seat in the chair, and Dr. Davies braced his own body against him. The doctor had not exaggerated. The roots of the wisdom teeth were curled under the jawbone, and he had to split the teeth, then pick them out. Brute strength was needed, and through his own pain, Jim could feel the palpitations of the dentist's heart.

After each tooth came out, Mrs. Mann would bring in a slug of home brew for Jim and one for the dentist. When the seven bad teeth had been pulled, Mrs. Mann and Pat King carried Jim to her guest room, where a steaming bath was waiting. They got him into the hot water, soaked him till he began to relax, then put him to bed. When he hit the pillow, Jim passed out cold.

15

Wolves in the Night

"We're going to leave here," Jim announced one evening. "I can't stand having you alone up here at the Head. It's much too dangerous."

"But I'm not afraid, Jim."

"That's just it," he said. "That makes it worse. You trust everyone and everything: white men, Indians, animals—even the grizzlies. It's not safe for you, dear."

"I know you worry about my safety; and I worry about you out alone on the trap line. But most of the time this is paradise, Jim, and I want to stay here forever—with you!"

"We've got to do something," he said desperately. "I won't be satisfied until we've moved back somewhere nearer civilization."

"Not too near, Jim."

Jim scouted up and down the ninety-mile Inlet, and finally ran across an Indian who had a registered trap line down near the mouth of the Inlet, a few hours' run from Alert Bay and Minstrel Island. A much better place, Jim was certain, for Laurette to be when he had to leave her alone. The boat traffic was much heavier, and she could hail someone in case of trouble. Since Jim's line was much better located, and had more animals on it than his, the Indian was delighted with the idea of trading.

"But I can't swap with you," he told Jim. "It has to go through the Indian agent at Alert Bay."

The Indian agent, Judge Holliday, said it would require a majority vote of the tribe, and called the Indians together. When he put the proposal to them, the man who owned the trap line jumped up and shouted "Yes!" but all the others voted "No."

"What are the objections?" the judge asked, puzzled.

A spokesman for the group rose. "We want the white couple to stay where they are."

"Why?"

"Because when we are sick, they take care of us. When we are in trouble, they help us. We need them. We do not want them to leave."

There was nothing Judge Holliday could do. Jim was stuck with his trap line and the dangerous, isolated life at the head of the Inlet.

The Indians and visitors had left the Inlet. It was time for the big freeze again and Jim was once more making preparations for trapping. One day the Game Warden appeared up at the Head, leading, somewhat shamefacedly, a scrawny, half-grown hound pup.

Jim looked at it with distaste. "A present?" he asked wryly. Sometimes it got to be a nuisance to have a reputation for being a soft touch.

"Yeah," the Warden said. "I was down at Glendale, checking the cannery after they closed for the season, and I found this pup. Belonged to some Indians, and they left him behind. I'm supposed to shoot 'em when I find them deserted like that. It's better than leaving them to die of slow starvation."

Jim looked at the starved bony pup. "Why didn't you?"

"I dunno," the Warden admitted. "I was going to, but there

was just something about him kept me from it. Thought I'd bring him up and see if you folks would like to have him."

"If the missus sees him, she'll probably keep him," Jim said. "She feeds anything. But now that we've got rid of our pigs, I'm not much of a mind to take on anything else. Winters are too rough here to have to look after anything besides yourself."

"Well," the Warden shrugged, "I'll just leave him and you can decide later. Kill him, if you want. But I remembered that Airedale of yours you were so fond of——"

"Growler? Growler was a *good* dog."

"I figured this one might be worth giving a chance," the Warden said. "You can't see much now, when he's starved down like this, but he's got some good dog in him. There was two hand loggers, up by Alert Bay, who got a bright idea and imported a pair of Kentucky cougar hounds. The dogs were guaranteed to go after cougar, but leave the deer alone."

"Did they?" asked Jim.

"Not exactly," laughed the Warden. "They chased all the deer off two islands before the boys got a chain on 'em. And they didn't touch a cougar!"

"Well," Jim said, "this isn't one of 'em!"

"No," the Warden admitted. "The loggers were so disgusted they killed 'em. But one of the pair had already got to a pedigreed pointer bitch some fancy English hunter had brought up to Alert Bay. When she had her pups, he gave 'em away to anybody that would take 'em. An Indian probably got this one."

"He may have had some fancy parents behind him, but he sure doesn't look like much himself!"

"Well, I probably should have killed him instead of bothering you with him," the Warden said. "I don't know what got into me."

"That's all right," Jim said. "Just get on down the Inlet before the missus comes back from her berrying. If she sees the scrawny cuss, she'll start feeding him."

Jim said good-by to the Warden, then looked down at the miserable pup beside him. Its large feet flapped dismally at the end of scrawny legs; he was a hound, for sure. Both rib and flank bones showed through, and his hair was a mat of burrs and stickers. His big sad eyes peered up at Jim questioningly.

"Might as well get it over," Jim muttered. "Come along."

He got his rifle out of the cabin and marched off into the woods, the skinny pup following him. The trail led into dense thicket. Suddenly the ludicrous, bony, big-footed hound pup sprinted past Jim up the trail—his nose high, his head poised —and picked up speed as he began working into the wind.

Fascinated in spite of himself, Jim followed him. Within a few feet the hound stopped, turned to signal and froze. Jim peered into the clearing before him; there stood a beautiful eight-point buck. Taking aim, Jim fired, and the buck fell. That was meat enough to last half the winter. As he gutted the carcass, and strapped the meat to his back to haul home, the hungry dog stood beside him, watching. When Jim came out of the woods that day, he brought back a dead deer and a dog that was very much alive.

Laurette was out in the woodshed getting a salt salmon from her brine crock to freshen for supper. She looked up in amazement. "Where did he come from?"

"Warden brought him," Jim explained. "He was deserted down at the cannery."

"Why, the poor pup! I'll get him something to eat right now." She hurried into the house, leaving the lid off the brine crock. Jim put down the deer carcass and began cutting out the meat. The hungry pup looked from Jim to the door in which Laurette had gone, then, making up his mind, ran to the crock, snatched out a whole six-pound salted salmon and dashed down the beach, away from the house.

Laurette came to the door with bannock and canned milk. "Oh, Jim," she cried, "get that away from him. He can't eat that salt fish—he'll die. It's got to be freshened first———"

"Too late now," Jim looked down to the beach where the pup had hauled his salmon to a safe distance from the house and was now ravenously devouring it. "He'll just get a little thirsty, that's all."

The hound quit eating as the salt took hold of his throat and belly. At the creek beside the spring, he drank great gulps of water; then panting with thirst, he waded into the creek, lapping water frantically. Finally, he got down on his belly so that his body was submerged, and, resting his face on a stone, lay there, only enough of his muzzle out of water so that he could breathe.

It was the last salt salmon that Scout, as they named him, ever ate.

A few days of Laurette's good feeding showed up promptly on the starved pup. As he lapped up canned milk, eggs, bannock, meat, his sides filled out, and within weeks his body had rounded and grown almost big enough to match his feet.

He was an ingratiating pup, and one of his strangest friends was Laurette's tomcat, lone survivor of the three from Kwalate. When Scout came in the house, wet and dirty after a day in the woods with Jim or out retrieving birds from the slew, the old tom would greet him with fatherly affection, purring a welcome. As soon as Scout lay down, the cat would set about washing and drying him and, with nightly lickings from the old cat, Scout's coat soon became well-kept and glossy.

At night, during the winter when there were no visitors or guests, Laurette and Jim got out their sheet music and sang to amuse themselves. Scout and the tomcat lay on the rug beside them. Though he was apt to sleep through some of their finest songs, Scout never failed to waken and join the chorus when they reached "Holy City." Jim and Laurette couldn't figure what that song meant to the dog; but every time they played it, Scout would waken, sit up and chime in, hauntingly howling the high notes along with them.

Scout was a natural-born hunter. He seemed to know exactly what his master wanted. If Jim took down his shotgun, Scout was ready to retrieve ducks, but if Jim reached for his rifle, Scout was set for deer, and he wouldn't have looked at a duck if it had sat on his nose.

Though a bird dog by instinct and heredity, Scout never bothered any of the pet grouse, partridge, or ducks that Laurette brought in to nurse through some injury or ailment. He seemed to make an immediate distinction between "pets" and "game."

For the first time Jim had a real partner on his trap line. Like Growler, Scout served as liaison between Jim and Laurette, When Jim was in his Mussel Lake cabin, he had only to pin a note to Scout's collar and say, "Go home, Scout," and the hound would light out toward home. On these missions nothing could stop him, not a deer or a bear—or even a wasp. He made the ten miles of trail in an hour and a half. Back home, Laurette would feed the dog, rest him, give him an answering note, and back he'd go—another hour and a half's run—to Jim.

Scout's value, however, was more than that of a companion and messenger. He ran the trap line with Jim, taking his place an even fifteen paces ahead of his master. When he encountered a bear, he would stop, turn, and signal to Jim. Jim would then take his pack off and get ready for action in case of trouble. If the bear seemed "okay," Scout would keep his eye on him as he and Jim crowded by. If the bear looked as though he wouldn't allow them to edge past, Jim would say, quietly, "Scout, take him away."

Scout would then run at the bear, and chase him. A grizzly hates dogs and will only chase for a while, then turn and charge. When the bear charged, as he always did, Scout would leap ahead of him and lead him off into the woods, then circle around and come back to Jim, "grinning," Jim swears, from ear to ear. Most dogs, when charged by a bear, turn tail and run back to their masters, bringing them "a lapful of bear."

At home, Scout stayed close to the cabin and made no effort to tangle with the grizzlies that grazed in the nearby flats. So long as they kept their peace, it was a live-and-let-live arrangement. Except for Peeping Tom.

Peeping Tom was too curious to keep his distance. A four-year-old red-coated male grizzly, he became fascinated, with the sight of Jim working on his gas-boat. Jim had loaned his boat to a man who let it beat on the beach until the ribs were cracked, and Jim's first spring job was to caulk it. As soon as it was warm enough to work outside, he put the gas-boat up on ways built at the top of the high-tide mark and crawled under to work. He was lying on his back, pounding oakum into the boat seams, when he suddenly had the odd sensation that he was being watched. He rolled over—and looked directly into the face of the big red grizzly, peering under the boat at Jim from a distance of eight feet. He stared curiously at Jim for a few minutes, then, apparently satisfied as to what Jim was doing, lumbered off a few feet and lay on the grass, with his head down so that he could see under the boat and watch the work.

This was too much for Scout. He made a furious barking charge and succeeded in running the bear off. But fifteen minutes later the big red grizzly was back again, peering under the boat, his face as friendly and interested as before.

Next morning he was back. Once again Scout ran him off. Fifteen minutes later he reappeared. This went on for several mornings, and finally Scout got tired of running him. The bear lay on his side of the boat, watching Jim work, and Scout lay on the other, his worried eyes on the grizzly to make sure he didn't start trouble.

He didn't. Each morning during the two weeks that Jim worked on his boat the bear walked over, got down where he could stick his huge head under, "smiled" at Jim, then settled down a few feet off where he could watch. In the afternoon, when hunger finally overcame his curiosity, Peeping Tom would wander over into the flats to dig some roots for his dinner. But next morning he was back—on the dot. He never made trouble—he simply liked to kibitz.

There was no game Scout would rather go after than the vicious timber wolves. These Siberian timber wolves that inhabit the glacial areas of British Columbia are incredibly big. One female wolf, taken near Jim's cabin, measured seven feet ten inches, over all.

During the winter, when a hard crust was frozen over the snow and they could hear the wolves' claws scratching on the surface, the eerie noise sent a shudder through Laurette, but it presaged excitement for man and dog. At the first sound Scout would get up and look hopefully at his master. Sometimes Jim would go to the door, open it, and howl to the wolves.

He has two wolf calls, the regular and the meat call. "I can't fool an old wolf, but the young ones will answer," he said. If the wolves replied and kept coming, he and Scout went out, the dog to decoy the wolves, Jim to shoot them.

Scout was able to outrun the big wolves until he was fourteen years old.

One afternoon Laurette followed them and hid behind a stump.

Scout ran up to the edge of the woods and yipped. Eight dog-wolves leaped out, and Scout whirled and rushed back to the spot where Jim was stationed with his gun, followed by the wolves which were powerful runners, and perilously close. As he came within Jim's range, Scout put on speed, one eye on Jim, the other on the wolves.

"I couldn't decide whether to hide my eyes or look," Laurette said. As each wolf gained on the dog, it would reach out to hamstring Scout's leg, lose a half-stride, fall a little behind, then gain again.

Bang! The first wolf, closest to Scout, went rolling to the ground "ass over teakettle," as Jim described it. Another shot, and Jim "knocked a front wheel off" the second comer, breaking it down with a shot into the front shoulder at a little over forty yards. A big black dog-wolf closed in on Scout, and Laurette hid her eyes. Bang!—and that wolf fell to the ground, its fangs inches from Scout's flying feet. Within minutes, Jim had knocked down four of the eight wolves; the other four made off into the timber. With one last shot in his gun chamber, Jim fired over a hundred yards away, and "damned if I didn't knock a front wheel off the last wolf I could see."

But Jim was afraid that some day the wolves would get Scout, as they had Growler. One night they almost did, by the old trick of sending in a female to lure the dog. A bitch wolf came in alone, near the Stantons' cabin, "talking nice," as Jim said, and lured the hound into following her out— where the dog wolves waited.

Scout was cagey and tried to stay close to the cabin, but a couple of the dog wolves sneaked in and caught him. Jim rushed out with his gun, but the melee of three wolves and a dog in the dark was too uncertain for a shot. Jim shot over the fighting pack, hoping to scare them. There was no use trying to light the wolves' eyes, for unlike any other animal in the woods, wolves won't look into a light. Finally the dog managed to break free and get into the house. He survived with a rip in his side and a bite on one leg.

The following summer Scout was outside with Laurette when a bitch wolf came near and called to him. Scout was off like a shot. Terrified, Laurette went after him, and found him cowering in the doorway of the house!

Scout had another enemy in the woods—wasps. Once on a hunting trip Jim sat down for a smoke, and Scout sat down companionably nearby—on top of an underground wasp hole. As the wasps met his back end, Scout leaped up, took off in a run, and didn't come back for some time. After that, it was open season on wasps. He tried to fight and kill every one he saw. And all Jim had to do to drive him crazy was say, "B-z-z-z."

Scout dearly loved ripe berries. Whenever he came upon a loaded bush, he would reach up, pull a branch down with his paw, and eat until he was full, or until Jim got ahead of him on the trail. At home he liked nothing better than to go out with Laurette and help her pick berries. One day when she was out after huckleberries, she heard Scout rustling through the brush beside her, but he never came close. "That dog," she thought, "is so busy eating he won't help me." When she returned to the cabin later, she was startled to see Scout asleep on the floor. He had obviously been there a long time. She looked behind her out the door and saw a big, old black wolf. She stared at the old wolf—and he stared back. She looked closer. The old fellow's teeth were worn down and he moved at a slow limp. Obviously he had become too old to hunt, and had left the pack of younger wolves. Now, mellowed by age, his only interest in life lay in begging a little food. When Scout awoke, at Laurette's call, he went outside, sniffed at the old wolf, and came back. Then Laurette carried food out to the old black wolf and he took it gratefully.

One of the strangest relationships in the wilderness is that of wolves and grizzlies. The male and female wolves, who share the responsibility of feeding their cubs, are the only animals who dare prey on the mammoth grizzly, and from cubhood, the only animal feared by the grizzly is the big timber wolf.

For every track of grizzly mother with cubs can be found a following wolf track. The wolves follow, then sneak up and capture a cub. The sow bear of course charges the wolf, but the wolf has already done his damage—hamstringing or fatally injuring the cub. All he has to do is sidestep the mother's charge and wait. Eventually she goes on, leaving the body of her cub—and the wolves come back. If they are close to their dens, they carry the meat in, or, if not, they simply settle down, gorge it, then go home and regurgitate the food for the pups' consumption.

Jim doubts that twenty full-grown wolves would be able to kill a two-year-old grizzly. But the bear fears the wolves until he gains maturity several years later.

As chronology advances, the situation oddly reverses. Natural enemies in earlier life, the old rascals join up in their advanced age to combine their talents in the constant struggle for survival. Just as for every track of mother and cubs, there is the trailing predatory wolf, Jim found that for every track of an old outsized boar grizzly, there is a companion wolf track. Using their joint talents, the two cronies work together for food and protection. The "guard" wolf, with his keener scent, can always detect man, and he gives the bear warning, which sends him scooting back into the protection of the dense forest. This, Jim says, is what makes the real trophy bear— the huge outsized old boar grizzly—so difficult to get. The bear has his wolf to guard him, and "you can't sneak up on a wolf!"

The wolf, in turn, is paid off for his guard by extra food. Though the wolf is a fair fisherman, the grizzly is superb. He catches fish and his wolf eats his leavings.

Carefully secreting himself, so that even the wary wolf would miss his scent, Jim has witnessed this phenomenal friendship many times. He has seen the wolf move out ahead and "case" the area while his bear moves behind him in the woods no more than a ripple in the willows. If the territory is safe, the wolf signals, and the big bear moves cautiously into the clearing. If the area is suspect, the wolf goes back, and they both disappear into the impenetrable brush. Only once has Jim been able to get a hunter close enough to observe this strange brotherhood. It is almost impossible for an animal—and very difficult for a man—to outsmart a wolf. "Every large city has its crime element," Jim said, "and in the wilderness it's the wolves."

16

"Do-It-Yourself"

Though Laurette never complained, Jim knew that she felt cramped in the one-room cabin, particularly since Jimmy Varley had come to live with them.

It was in the depths of the Great Depression in the early thirties, when many families were finding it hard to make ends meet, and Jimmy's mother, the sole support of her large brood, had all she could do to keep her family together. Jimmy had come to the Inlet with a mountain-climbing party. He was a slender, sensitive youngster, and the Stantons had promptly taken him into their hearts.

Laurette and Jim had never been completely reconciled to their childlessness, but since there was nothing they could do about it, it was a secret thing that they never spoke of. Then one quiet, peaceful evening Laurette opened her heart to Jim.

"Jimmy Varley," she began, "is an awfully nice boy. Too bad that he has to go back to town."

"Yes," Jim agreed. "It must be tough on his mother to take care of all those children. And hard on Jimmy, too, with no jobs anywhere."

"You and I both had fine foster parents, Jim. Remember how Evan Evenson taught you to be a good hunter and trapper?"

"I sure do."

"Jimmy Varley could help you with the hunting parties now, and in the winter he could go out on the trap lines."

"It wouldn't be so gosh-awful lonesome then."

"Let's ask him to stay on with us, Jim."

"Well," he said thoughtfully, "sometimes it's hard to feed two mouths, let alone three."

"Goodness!" Laurette exclaimed. "When there's a big freeze, we feed half the Indians in the territory, it seems, in addition to any strangers who might happen along."

"Of course, if you want the boy . . ."

The next day they spoke to Jimmy Varley, and he enthusiastically accepted their invitation, with the proviso that he could leave, if he wished, any time a boat was running.

Jimmy quickly adapted himself to the rugged life of the woods and soon proved invaluable as a helper with the hunting parties. He was an alert youngster with a quiet good humor and a natural aptitude for camp cooking, a job Jim had never cared for. At home Jimmy was a willing chore boy for Laurette, and his youthfully high spirits matched her own.

Nearly eight years had gone by in the cabin at the Head, and since the time he had panicked after his sickness, Jim had had no doubt that they would spend the rest of their lives in the wilderness. Their cash box was never full; still, with his trap lines and the hunting parties that came to the Head, it was never empty now, either.

The land around them and part way down the Inlet belonged to a family in Vancouver who had inherited it after the dissolution of the German colony. Though nothing was being done with it, the owners seemed to have little desire to sell—the price they asked was, for the Stantons' modest savings, prohibitive. Finally, a small piece of land, about twenty acres, two miles down the slew from their cabin, was let go by the estate for taxes, and became the property of the government. As soon as Jim heard the news, he told Laurette his plans.

"I'd love a big place," she said. "One-room cabins are cozy, but that's about all you can say for them."

"I'm not sure yet whether we can swing it, you know," Jim said doubtfully. "If the land takes most of our savings, I haven't figured out a way to get the money to build the house."

"I know," Laurette exclaimed, "we'll have a log house!"

"That's an idea. We'll hand-log the trees ourselves. Then all we'll need to buy is finished lumber for the floor and trim, and the hardware."

"Let's start right now," Laurette said enthusiastically, "and draw up the plans for a really big house!"

"First," Jim reminded her, "we've got to get the land."

By early January they knew the property would be theirs and determined to have the house built and ready to move into by fall. The size and structure would have to be limited by their physical capabilities. Jim, Laurette, and Jimmy together could not take the place of tractors and cement mixers; yet they wanted it big and comfortable.

"I know one thing we're going to have in that house," Jim firmly announced to Laurette and Jimmy.

"A bedroom?"

"Oh, we'll partition off rooms," Jim said, "but what I'm thinking of is an old-fashioned, honest-to-God fireplace! Not one of those dinky little holes in the room like those we have in our trapping cabins. I mean a huge, fine-drawing fireplace —big enough to take five-foot logs and heat a whole house." Jim settled back in his chair. "I've been dreaming of it for years—and, by damn, I'm going to have it now!"

"You think we can build one that size by ourselves?" Laurette said doubtfully.

"Sure," said Jim. "I can even do it alone. I've studied every fireplace I've seen, and I know just what they've got to have and exactly how I'm going to make ours."

Laurette laughed. "All right, honey," she said, "but first we'll need some walls to put around it."

The twenty acres lay around the curve of Dutchman's Head, an untouched stretch of forest, extending from the mountain above down to the edge of the water, with the heavier cedar and fir trees giving way to scraggling alders near the high-tide line. The narrow stretch of beach was covered with marsh grass and mud where the tide came in, and was littered with large skeletal branches of driftwood.

The house, which would stand above tide level, would be built of logs from the beautiful cedar trees which grew on the other side of the Inlet, where they had hand-logged in their Kwalate days. Jim ordered the sawn wood for the flooring and window casings from a mill ninety miles away; glass for the windows and doors, hardware and carpentry supplies, and a well pump had to be ordered from Vancouver.

On the first of April they loaded their food supplies into the gas-boat, moved down to the building site, set up living quarters in a tent, and went to work.

First the land had to be cleared of trees and brush. In ten days they chopped down thirty-five alder trees and dug out the roots. When the trees were out, they began digging a well, and found that they had to go through a hardpan. Working at top speed, Jim and Jimmy could dig out no more than eight inches a day.

The entire project had to be completed by mid-October, when the first freeze came, so, while the men worked on the stubborn well, Laurette cleared brush, then began packing the boat with the gear they would need for hand logging. Two weeks later they were on their way across the Inlet to select the trees for their log house. Jim chose a grove of cedars high on the side of the mountain, where they could be stumped into the water below. He chopped the undercuts, and Laurette and Jimmy hauled up the saws and jacks they would need. When Jim had the first tree ready to saw, and the springboard in place, Laurette clambered up onto a board, saw in hand.

"Get down. I don't want you hand logging," Jim said, remembering the gossip of long ago. "You can pack supplies for Jimmy and me."

"Jimmy doesn't know how to use the springboard," Laurette pointed out. "Besides, we aren't hand logging, we're building our own house!"

"Well, all right." Jim glanced apprehensively at Laurette, no longer a young woman, on her precarious perch. Saw in hand, eyes glistening, she looked down at the green forest world which swept away below her.

"Come on," she shouted, "let's get going!"

When they had felled about thirty-eight trees, they barked them, slid them into the Inlet, and towed them, whole, across the Inlet on high tide. Then they rolled the logs ashore with a peevy, leaving them out to season and dry.

Making a run down to Glendale, they picked up the glass, cement, hardware, and door. Everything had arrived except the well pump.

The house was to be a long, low structure, twenty by forty feet, the maximum size, Jim felt, that could be heated by a single fireplace, and built without machinery. With the later addition of a roofed woodshed on the kitchen end, it would be twenty by sixty feet, over all.

There would be no basement foundation. There was no time for it, anyway. They laid a sill of 44-foot-long cedar logs, placed on cedar blocks. A cross-sill every two feet would carry the floor.

One day a scow appeared along the Inlet, and dropped nine thousand feet of lumber at the beach!

"You're Stanton, aren't you?" the scow man asked. "Mr. Spicher told me to drop this here. I'm taking the rest of the load to his camp."

Bob Spicher was a logging friend who was opening a camp fourteen miles down the Inlet. He had gone to Vancouver to buy a scow-load of equipment, and knowing that Jim was building a house, had ordered the lumber sent up on his scow. He figured Jim would be needing it about the time it arrived. His inspiration had saved Jim the laborious task of hauling lumber in his small boat and nearly four days of valuable time.

Then a seemingly insuperable problem presented itself. It had been work enough to roll the 44-foot logs ashore with peevies. It had not occurred to them that rolling them up on top of each other, horizontally, to make the walls was more of a job than they could handle.

"How about cutting them the height of the house?" Laurette suggested. "Then stand them up, side by side."

Jim studied a minute. "Don't know as I've ever seen a house built with the logs placed vertically, but I can't see anything wrong with it."

After careful figuring and measuring, they sawed the logs to 8½-foot lengths, the height of the house. With a broadax they smoothed the inside half of each log to form the interior walls.

Jim had just begun to smooth the broadax marks out of the wood with his plane when a man in a small boat stopped alongshore to ask directions. He watched Jim work for a few minutes, then laughed and shook his head.

"What's wrong?" Jim asked belligerently.

"Nothing," the man said with a grin. "I was just thinking what a funny world this is. I been working on summer houses for some rich folks over at Vancouver Island, and they're paying a fellow good money just to put those ax marks back in so it'll look rustic. And here you are, sweating to get 'em out."

Jim stared at the man, then smiled and put down his plane. "Thanks," he said. "I think we'll look rustic, too! Particularly, running behind time as we are."

They attacked each log with ropes, pulled it over beside the sill, set the base end, pulled it up slowly into place, stockade fashion, and toenailed it temporarily with long spikes. As each log was pulled up, Jim ran a saw down the edge that touched the previous one, then shoved the two together so that each log fitted snugly against its neighbor.

Working in this laborious fashion, they couldn't handle more than four or five of the big logs a day. By the time they had the four walls up, they had pulled 140 heavy logs into place—a formidable, almost impossible, task for three people, one of them a diminutive woman—and another month had gone by.

They were exhausted and needed rest, but they couldn't afford to stop for a minute. They even worked by lantern light far into the night, but at dawn, after a sketchy breakfast, they were at it again.

One day Jimmy stopped for a second to wipe the sweat from his eyes.

"Oh, shucks, we'll be done in plenty of time." He hoped to bring Laurette back to her usual optimistic self, but it was no use, for she, like Jim, realized the impossibility of their undertaking.

"Where's that damned pump?" she said. Laurette rarely

swore—that was Jim's province—but when she did, it was a sign that she was at the breaking point.

"Haven't got time to think about it now, dear," Jim said, glancing at her anxiously.

Laurette suddenly threw down the ax she was using and burst into tears. Jim silently went on with his work. There wasn't even time to think about her.

After the wall logs had been drawn up and forced together, Jim temporarily caulked the open seams with oakum. The following year, after the logs had shrunk, and the house settled, he would drive the caulking in tight and cover the seams with cedar strips.

Meanwhile, Laurette and Jimmy began splitting cedar shakes for the roof. They used old-fashioned shake frows, iron wedges which are placed on top of the sawed surface of a short log, then driven down with a heavy wooden club, so that thin, shinglelike widths of wood are split off.

By the time they had the shakes cut, the roof laid, and Jim had run cement around the base of the logs to bugproof the house, it was late September and already the temperature was at freezing. A sharp wind became increasingly bitter. An early and rugged winter was obviously on its way.

Jim set all the windows in one day, hand-hewing the casings with his broadax. In another day he laid the thousand feet of flooring, which Jimmy handed to him as he worked.

The first of October, with the thermometer registering zero, they moved into their new house. It was a barn with windows! No fireplace nor partitions. Jim had set a big drum heater, with a cooker top, in the middle of the room and they huddled around it.

It was like the first winters at Kwalate, sixteen years ago. They had no cash left, and Jim had to get out on his trap line.

He, Jimmy, and Scout took off, but by early December they were forced to give up. The first of November had brought seven feet of snow—and they were in the throes of an old-fashioned "freeze in" on the Inlet. They would be broke again until spring.

During the freeze Jim erected the partitions, separating the twenty- by forty-foot barn into a large living room, an open kitchen-dining area, and two bedrooms. But the intense cold kept them from enjoying their new, luxurious privacy. Jim and Laurette's bed as well as Jimmy's cot stayed right where they were, in the big room, all winter, drawn up alongside the big drum stove.

At the first sign of thaw Jim went to work patiently collecting material for the fireplace: railroad iron hauled from a deserted mine, fox wire, and rocks. He had to go a quarter-mile from the beach, above the high-water mark, to get rocks; water-soaked rocks from below tide level would blow up when the fire was lit. He made stretchers by putting handles on wooden milk cases, loaded these with rock, and brought them, by water, to the beach in front of the new house. His punt would carry nearly a ton of rock each trip.

By the time Jim's fireplace was finished, he had used 1½ tons of sand and 15 tons of rock. He had laid the front rocks carefully to form a beautiful design across the face of his masterpiece. Finished, the giant fireplace measured 7½ feet, over all, with a depth of 4 feet. It was literally a stand-up fireplace, or at least a sit-in one for adults, and would consume logs of four or five feet. So that they would not have a smoky room when the wind was wrong, Jim built a smoke shelf 12 inches back, with a 16-inch opening. When a down draft occurred, the smoke hit the shelf and was sent back up the chimney.

A few days after Jim had completed it, Charlie Panquit came to call. He sat down facing the new fireplace. For a full hour he stared intently into the fire; then he turned to Jim and said, "What the matter, no smoke?"

Years later, when an earthquake shook the northern coast of British Columbia, it shattered every chimney in that section except Jim's. His fireplace survived with but a single crack.

The upright logs, Laurette discovered to her delight, were easy to keep clean. Instead of accumulating in crevices, the dirt and dust fell from the top to the base, where it could easily be removed; and later, Jim found the vertical structure invaluable from another standpoint. If one of the logs was eaten by lumber ants and rotted, he had only to remove that log and split it, blow-torch the ants out, fill the log with cement, and put it back together like an eclair, then replace it in the wall.

The pump finally arrived a year late. By then they had money enough to paint the exterior logs of the house a rich forest green. When the logs had properly settled, and Jim had driven the oakum in permanently and covered the inside with cedar strips. Laurette went to work on the interior. She hand-varnished every log in the house, until the inside walls, from kitchen through living room and bedrooms, gleamed in their natural beauty.

Jim had been so busy finishing the interior, as well as attempting to accumulate a little cash, that he could not find time to build the projected shed. However, in the second spring in the new house a party of young men turned up on the Inlet and Jim put them to work.

The boys, rather than go on relief, had banded together and come into the woods, hoping to earn a livelihood by prospecting in the mountains. By the time they appeared at the Inlet, they had a couple of weeks' supply of food left but no money, and no way of buying steamer passage. When their food ran out, Laurette, of course, began feeding them. When they had built the woodshed, three of the boys found work with a logger who had come into the Inlet that spring, and the fourth boy, Jack Clark, stayed on with the Stantons.

Jimmy Varley had gone back to his mother in Vancouver, and Jim was on the alert for good help, since he was guiding more and more hunters. Jack Clark was older than Jimmy and basically an outdoorsman. He had been a prairie cowboy, at one time washed gold on the Fraser River, and was at home either in the woods or on a boat. Jim offered him a third of the profits from his trap line, as well as food and all expenses, in exchange for his help.

For once the trap line paid off, and during the five years that Jack lived with the Stantons, he was able to put aside enough so that he could, at Jim's urging, buy a trap line of his own and his own gas-boat. Four weeks after he went into business for himself, Jack had $750 worth of furs. Eventually he made enough to buy a $7,500 boat. From that beginning, he went on to a successful career.

17

Grizzlies For Sale

Still needing cash, Jim and Laurette spent the summer of 1946 gill-netting on the Inlet. That year loggers moved up to the Franklin River, at the Head, a mile from their house. Most of the grizzlies faded deep into the woods when they found the logging camps in operation on their old feeding grounds, but one sow bear, who lived on the flats in the Franklin River, with three first-year cubs trailing her, decided to make a stand against the intrusion. She stayed around the camp, charging anyone who came near her and wrecking everything she could get her heavy paws on. She was an ornery bear, a "mustache grizzly," the Indians called her.

The loggers were finally forced to kill the sow to avoid further trouble; but some of the men took pity on the three nursing-age cubs, brought them into camp, and fed them on warm milk. As they got older, they ate everything the men would give them but hotcakes were their special favorite, and by the end of the summer each cub could easily consume fifty at a sitting.

The problem was what to do with them after they grew up. Or, more immediately, what to do with them when the camp closed down for the winter and the loggers went to town. Knowing the Stantons' reputation for kindness, the men asked them if they would take on the feeding of their cubs, and Laurette agreed to go over to the camp every other day and leave out feed for the bears. She also asked the boys before they left for town to place a big, easily read sign on the beach, stating that these bears were PETS and asking hunters not to shoot them. The young loggers made the sign and posted it, wrote a letter to Stanley Park in Vancouver to see if they wanted the cubs, and left the Inlet.

Every other day Jim and Laurette got in their gas-boat and took food over to the babies. After their summer diet of hotcakes and milk, the triplets were rolling fat and happy, and completely unafraid of humans. One of the cubs, Ring, the female, was an especially fine specimen of grizzly, in that she bore the rare, ringed-neck marking.

Knowing the size and strength the cubs would attain at maturity, neither Jim nor Laurette ever encouraged them to become too familiar. At close quarters, they always carried something to divert the bears, a morsel of food or a plaything that held their attention. But a few weeks later, nearing home in the gas-boat, Laurette suddenly grasped Jim's arm. The three little bears were running along the beach, trailing after the boat. To have come this far the cubs had had to cross a swift river and make their way along a steep wooded bank, but they had made up their collective mind that there was no point in being stranded down at the deserted logging camp when they could come home with the folks who fed them.

From that time on, the three bears lived in the Stantons' yard, played on their beach—and scared the living daylights out of their visitors.

The triplets were beautiful to look at, and each had a personality of his own. Ring was the most playful of the group, Joe the shyest, and Shorty the racketeer. When food was put out, Shorty would slyly shout "Woof woof" and gallop off into the woods, leading his brother and sister. Then, losing them, he would make a wild dash back—and get the best of the food for himself before they discovered the trick.

Late that summer General Robert Woods came to the Inlet on a fishing trip. Among his party was a man from the Brookfield Zoo who, when he saw the three fine specimens—one a rare, ring-necked bear—immediately offered to take them. Laurette and Jim were delighted. Their young grizzlies would have good food and the best of care the rest of their lives. Feeding them indefinitely was a problem, and the cubs' lack of early training in forest survival made their lives hazardous. The zoo seemed the perfect solution.

Laurette wrote to the loggers, and they agreed to let the bears go. Arrangements were begun to ship the animals, but the matter had to await clearance through the British Columbia Game Department. Jim agreed, when it was cleared, to build cages in which to ship the bears; then, with Laurette, to accompany them to Chicago, feeding and caring for them in transit.

Working out the details of the shipment and getting permission from the Game Department was, however, an involved process which dragged on the rest of the season. As fall approached, and hibernation time, the cubs began wandering over the surrounding area, and the scent of a garbage dump at one of the logging camps drew them. Though logging operations were closed down, the owner of the camp was staying on through the winter. Over his radio-phone he had heard the arrangements being made to ship the bears, and saw an opportunity to profit from the deal. He offered to donate whatever lumber would be needed to build the cages.

Jim accepted the offer and went up to the camp. It took him four days to build the three cages, which he had designed out of his knowledge of bear-nature. Constructed of heavy lumber, they had drop doors, and in the front of each cage was a "gnawing place"—a square hole faced with galvanized tin, and nail ends sticking through.

When the cages were ready, and the permissions were in order, Jim called to the three cubs. They obediently walked inside, and he dropped the doors. Each cub promptly started gnawing at the hole in front of his nose, then in a few minutes, gave it up as a bad deal. Jim went behind the cages, reached in and patted the cubs' hindquarters to quiet them, talking to them soothingly the while. They soon became calm and settled down on the floor of their cages.

The owner of the logging camp called the Brookfield Zoo on his radio-phone and reported that Jim was ready to start with his bears. What Jim did not know was that he also told the Zoo officials that he would send the bears only on condition that they pay him $1,500, $500 for each cub. Thinking that Jim, who had been left responsible for the shipment, was blackmailing them, the Zoo officials refused.

Jim and Laurette were ready for the big trip when word came that the deal was off. Jim immediately wrote, explaining the situation, but in the meantime he could do nothing but release the bears. When he opened the drop doors, Shorty, Ring, and Joe tumbled out, went over and rolled in the snow, then strolled back to their cages, walked inside, and went to sleep.

It was already late fall, and there was no chance that an answer could come back that season. The cubs went into hibernation in the woods, and in the spring, when they came out of hibernation and headed back for the Stantons', some loggers shot at them as they trotted along the beach. Shorty and Joe were killed; Ring escaped and made her way home.

She arrived, terrified by the shooting, miserable without her brothers, and in need of sympathy and affection. The three had been inseparable—if one left, even for a little while, the other two would cry. And now Ring was alone in the world.

Though she still trusted Laurette and Jim, and felt safe with them, she ceased to trust any other humans. She hated guns, loud noises, strange boats and strange people.

Ring tried to make a playmate out of Scout, who wanted no part of her. Scout was proud of his ability to lead off grizzlies from Jim, and when Ring trailed him, making playful passes, he would turn on her, get her by her stomach and roll her around. To his disgust, she considered this fun and always came back for more.

When Scout eluded her, Ring played with anything she could find. She loved anything that rattled; several times she took an oar lock out of the rowboat and ran off with it. If Jim made the mistake of leaving a coil of rope outside, she enjoyed taking one end and heading up for the mountains, the long rope playing out behind her. Sometimes it took Jim days to find his gear and tools.

Ring had a special passion for Jim's double-bitted ax, which she would pick up by its handle in her mouth, then run round and round the yard, like a zany woodcutter in search of a tree.

When she could find nothing to play with, or rattle, Ring liked to go down to the water, climb in the rowboat, and rock. She would sit there by the hour, gently rocking back and forth, like Whistler's "Mother" at sea.

Laurette insists that Ring enjoyed a view. She would sit on the shore for several hours, staring at a particularly lovely stretch of snow-capped mountains. Often they found her gazing dreamily into the water. Down on the beach at low tide she enjoyed lying on her back in the shallow water and tossing rocks or seaweed or driftwood into the air and trying to catch them. When they played the radio or piano in the house, she always wandered up to listen.

At five each morning Ring came to the back door to await breakfast. To keep her amused, Laurette would sometimes give her an empty jam tin. This simple toy might divert Ring for half a day. First she wiped out all the remnants of jam with her paws, licked them, and wiped again until not a smidgen of jam remained. Then she played with the empty tin, tossing it in the air as a child would a ball.

Laurette dug a hole out in the yard, big enough to hold a large pot, so that Ring wouldn't spill her food. The cub would eat out of the pot for a while; then, catching it in her mouth, she would lift it out and spill it, eat the remainder of her food off the grass, clean out the pot, and finally, turn her fat behind and sit down over the hole in the ground, as a child might whose schedule is food and potty.

They bought moldy bread at the cannery, which they gave Ring along with bannock, eggs, milk, and fish. She would fastidiously tear off the store wrapper, then eat the bread, or, if she was already full, she would leave the wrapper on, carry the loaf back into the woods, and cache it for a future meal.

Ring had a taste for fruit as well as bread, and one day she discovered a tree in the yard which bore green Italian plums. She found that if she shook the tree, the plums would fall off; then she could go around and gather them up. After that, Ring was always expectant. Every time she came to a new tree along the trail, she would shake it and watch to see if anything fell.

When Jim and Laurette went off in their boat, Ring trailed them along the beach for quite a way, shaking the trees as she walked along. When they returned, she hustled down to the beach to meet them, just as the pigs and cats had done.

If Jim had been fishing, Ring was especially anxious to

meet him, and, while he was tying up, would jump into the boat and start hunting for the fish heads he always saved her. Late that summer, when Laurette went out to gather raspberries for her season's canning, she found Ring asleep in the patch and not one berry left anywhere.

Whenever Jim went down to the beach to saw wood, Ring joined him, climbing companionably on one end of the log to watch him work. Her sociability, though a delight to the Stantons, was pretty hard on their guests. One man, the manager of a large corporation with interests in the Inlet, who habitually stayed with the Stantons on his yearly inspection tour, was in the outhouse when Ring decided to investigate. When her curious face appeared around the partition, he attempted to chase her off while maintaining a death grip on his trousers. He finally bolted past her to the house, his dangling trousers clutched around his legs.

That summer Ring had a gentleman caller, a male grizzly who stayed secreted in the woods back of the house until nightfall. Then he strode boldly in for his rendezvous, stepping through the flower garden and "setting the pansies back a month" with each step. Since Ring was barely two years old and did not have her full growth, this courtship was evidence that the grizzly may breed before maturity. Her cubs would have been born the following spring, before she had reached three years of age.

But that fall Ring went into hibernation and did not reappear the following spring. There was no indication that she had been shot. An orphaned cub without a mother's training, perhaps she had failed to eat blue clay, had gone into hibernation full of tapeworms, and died in her den.

18

The Private Life of a Grizzly

Over the years grizzlies have never failed to fascinate Jim. He confesses that he has devoted many hours that might have been spent in gainful occupation to studying their habits and acquiring the knowledge of them that has made him the world's outstanding authority on grizzlies.

Laurette, however, has never begrudged him this pleasure, though she says, "Sometimes I wondered whether Jim wasn't more interested in grizzlies than in me."

She shared some of his interest and enjoyed watching with him when she could, but household tasks and taking care of her beloved other animals absorbed most of her time.

Jim trailed the grizzlies alone—hunters made too much noise and Scout was of no use. The fear that the grizzly has of the wolf is so great that even a small dog can make a grizzly run in thoughtless terror, though he might eventually turn and charge.

Female grizzlies begin denning up in late October, and are usually out of sight by the end of November. They give birth to one, two, or three cubs every other year, in late February or early March, after a ten-month gestation. The young female grizzly, at two or three years of age, bearing her first young, never produces more than one cub. Generally her second pregnancy, two years later, will net two cubs, and many sows in the prime of life bear three cubs every two years.

The cubs are born blind, helpless, and tiny, weighing from one half to two pounds, and are practically hairless. Their eyes open after nine or ten days, but the mother doesn't risk bringing them out of the den until April or May, when the weather is mild and vegetation has started to grow. That summer the mother stays with her cubs, then takes them into her den again the following fall. Next summer the two-year-old trails her around, but the mother manages to get away from it long enough to breed. Then her problem is to get rid of the two-year-olds before she dens for the winter, when she will again produce cubs.

The sows begin driving off their cubs in September. Not understanding the physical cycle which makes the weaning necessary, the two-year-olds toddle up to Mama and get a slap across the face for their pains. The sow bear's methods are direct and to the point; a single blow sends her unwanted child thirty or forty feet. If there are twins, the other cub goes up to her, and gets a taste of the same thing, which sends him rolling on the ground, bellowing mightily, after which he usually sits up with a look of pained surprise. One sow, pursued by her cubs, would run to the slew, climb in and swim half a mile, then run along the bank, then swim again, finally outdistancing her small fry.

Jim has seen a mother who hadn't the heart to get rid of her first brood; she appeared, worn and tired, with two sets of cubs: her two-year-olds and the babies. Humanlike, she must have been too fond of her offspring to send them out alone into the cold world.

In Jim's country all the grizzlies den above the rain belt at 2,000 feet above sea level. Usually they make their beds under an overhanging rock, pulling in leaves to make a nest, then raking up more debris to cover the front entrance. When the snow falls, covering the den, the heat from the animal's body thaws an airhole in the roof, through which he breathes. All female grizzlies den up, and stay denned, since they are either caring for one-year-old cubs at this time or carrying cubs that will be born in the spring. But the males, Jim says, in spite of what has been written about them in nature books, den or not, as they choose and as the weather dictates. They stop along the river bars or cottonwood thickets, dig a hole in the ground and let the snow cover them, and sleep for a week or two, get up and prowl for a few days, then sleep again.

Jim has found fresh bear tracks on the twenty-seventh of February when the sun was shining and the bears had come out to stretch and prowl. For some reason he has never figured out, the higher the bears den up in the mountains, the later they appear the following spring.

Jim has observed the same grizzly going back to the same den for two years in succession, and in summer the adult bears maintain the same day bed, although the younger bears use different beds. One summer Jim counted forty-two summer beds along four miles of river, which he thought meant several beds for each bear. The bears establish these day beds so that they can see downhill, and the draft from the top of the hill warns of danger from above.

Though the grizzly generally begins turning in when cold weather comes, with the females preceding the males, Jim has found that no bear, male, female, grizzly or black, will go into hibernation until he has reached his maximum weight. One winter he observed a scrawny bear who stayed out, actively, most of the winter, feverishly digging for food. Jim would come out to shoot ducks and stand near the bear in the snow, but the frenzied bear would neither give up his digging nor run off. Jim believed that the bear had been shot, received some sort of injury, or was diseased. Something had obviously kept him from achieving his necessary weight.

One day Jim came up to a log, where a little skinny bear was lying asleep. Jim studied him leisurely. He was literally nothing but a bag of bones, though covered with luxuriant black fur. One paw was turned up as he slept, and Jim saw that the pad was worn down so that the bone showed through. Obviously the little bear was ill, and Jim decided to shoot him. One shot finished off the emaciated little fellow as he slept. Jim reached over the log and picked him up; he was so thin that the body was feather-weight. Jim carried the bear home, skinned the fur, which was in prime condition, and eventually gave it to a friend for a rug.

It is known that in hibernation, the body temperature of the bear drops, its respiration decreases, and the heart action slows down, but Jim decided to find out just how comatose this condition was. He knew the winter den of a grown sow and waited until she was well entrenched. Then when the wind was right so that no scent went to her, he sneaked by her den. The hibernating bear, unable to smell him, did, however, hear him, and got up and came out—proving that her faculties were not completely dulled.

The hibernating bear can exist without food. Even the boars, who don't stay denned up, don't seem to be hungry as they roam around throughout the winter.

When the bear comes out of his den in the spring, he wears the coat he went in with, which includes the layers of fat. Because he is not hungry, he stays near his den for four or five days, walking around, exercising, getting his bowels and kidneys regulated again. The lower bowel of the grizzly is thirty-five to forty feet long (the human's is twenty-five feet). While they are denned, this organ is dormant; the contents of the bowel become hardened, and at the base of the bowel is a plug, a dry mat of grass which must come out before the bowel is cleaned. When, after a few days of exercise, the bear gets rid of his plug, the bowel empties, and for several days he is "bathroom busy," making great piles of manure and urinating freely.

Now the bear begins to get hungry and his appetite seems to increase as summer goes on. He eats constantly, night and day, until he goes back into hibernation the following fall.

A grizzly appears in different places at various times of the year, ranging over an area of about forty miles, for his sleeping, fishing, and berrying. When the grizzly begins eating, he starts with a few bites of grass. A few days on that light diet, and he begins digging for skunk cabbage, which acts as a conditioner for his urinary tract and liver, and gets him in shape for the long summer meal ahead.

When the inner bear is cleansed, he starts getting rid of his itchy winter fur. He finds a likely rubbing tree, scratches it until it bleeds pitch, then rubs his neck in the pitch to get off the extra fur. Some favorite rubbing trees are used year after year. Two weeks of this and the bear is a sight to behold. His fur is matted with pitch, his neck and skin are rubbed raw and spotted with open sores and festered patches.

After he has shed the hot old coat, the bear quits rubbing on trees and does nothing to spoil the beauty of his new fall fur. But Jim used to call Laurette out to see one bear who came out on the flats each year. When he shed, he lost every vestige of fur except for the ridiculous lionlike roach on his neck. The Mexican Hairless, as Laurette called this unfortunate fellow, would stand around the flats, grazing in full view of the other bears, apparently not in the least embarrassed by his indecent appearance.

A phenomenon which fascinated Jim each spring as the

boars came out of hibernation, was "the tromp," as he called it. Moving down the trails and pausing beside the rubbing trees to scratch their necks, they also began working out the kinks in their muscles, limbering up their legs in a standing run, rocking, stamping, and moving their legs without going forward, like track athletes warming up at the starting line. Twenty-five to thirty yards on each side of the rubbing trees, Jim found the tromp holes worn into the trails.

Jim has watched this performance many times, but only after the most cautious of approaches, for the grizzly, standing there tromping his legs, is unusually alert and wary. His head sways as he moves, his nose sniffs the air for any stray scent. Grizzlies are so wary at this stage that Jim has never been able to bring a hunter close enough to observe a tromping bear.

By the middle of May the bears are moving down to the flats, digging wild rhubarb roots. They busy themselves with roots, salmonberry leaves and berries for the next couple of months. Though he wants fresh meat later on when his appetite reaches gargantuan proportions, the grizzly does not seem particularly interested in meat when he begins eating. Twice, for an experiment, Jim baited the grizzlies with seal when they first appeared on the flats, and was ignored, though a month or so later they couldn't get enough.

By mid-July they go down to the fishing streams every three or four days. In the meantime any carrion that they come across, they promptly consume—a dead mountain goat, carried down a snow slide, a dead sea lion washed up on the beach. It took three grizzlies ten days to eat one sea lion on the beach in front of the cabin.

When the fish arrive, both oolichan and salmon, the bears go on an exclusive fish diet. The grizzly wants his fish fresh; yet this diet physics him and also produces tapeworm. A greater enemy to the grizzly than hunters or Indians, the tapeworm takes a terrible toll; and the only grizzlies that survive are those who learn from their mothers the practice of eating blue clay. The worms get caught fast in the clay and are excreted with it. During fishing season Jim finds blue clay droppings all along the bank, with dead tapeworms enmeshed in them.

Unlike the oft-pictured bear standing midstream and flipping out fish with his paw, the grizzly actually catches the fish with his mouth, and carries each one out to shore, where he eats it. Early in the season, when fish are still scarce, the bear fishes carefully, working along three or four hundred yards of creek and feeling down under submerged logs. When his paw contacts a fish, he clamps it against the log, bends down and bites back of the fish's head. Then, reappearing above the water with the fish in his mouth, he wades ashore and settles down for his feast.

The grizzlies catch salmon which have already spawned, since the fish are slower then and easier to catch. The Fisheries Department once considered killing off the grizzly because they thought the bear was ruining the salmon crop. Jim and Dr. J. W. Bowers, of Fort Wayne, Indiana, opened several hundred salmon that grizzlies had caught, and out of that large number they found no more than a cupful of eggs. This discovery Jim reported to the Fisheries Department.

When he catches his first salmon of the season, the hungry grizzly eats all of the fish, leaving nothing more than a few scales and the intestines, which he pulls out to avoid the gall. But as the season progresses and fish are more plentiful, he eats only a few choice bites and then goes back for a fresh fish.

The cubs, like so many little boys, get such a kick from fishing that they soon quit eating their catch and simply haul out every fish they find for the sheer sport of it.

One day Jim sat down on the bank of the river near his punt to rest a moment. A grizzly came up the river, fishing in about a foot of water. A couple of salmon ran ahead of the bear and hid under Jim's punt. The grizzly followed them, apparently undisturbed by his human audience, searched along under the punt with his paw until he found one of the fish, clamped it, stuck his head down and got it in his mouth, then rose out of the water and headed across the stream. He climbed out on the opposite shore, and just before he disappeared into the woods with his dinner, he turned around, the fish still clamped in his mouth, faced Jim, and made a perfect little bow, as if to say, "Well, sir, that's the way I do it." Then he disappeared into the woods.

When the berries start ripening, the grizzlies start eating them, pulling down the bushes, eating leaves, berries, and all. Then back they go to fishing. As the season advances, the bears go up into the mountains where the berries are just ripening and then, Jim believes, they come back for more fish, though the accepted theory is that they lay off fish entirely and fill their stomachs with grass and leaves just before going back into hibernation. Jim's reason for thinking they return is simply the tracks he has seen, running back and forth from the berry line down to the fishing spots.

In fact, during the summer the grizzly will eat whatever is available: fish, meat, berries, grubs or bees, yellow jackets, bugs and mice. In Jim's country the main diet is salmon and berries. Studying bear droppings to analyze their diet, Jim has sometimes found deer hair and goat hair, but it is likely that these animals were consumed as carrion. Jim has seen grizzlies charge deer, but the deer easily outrun the bears, though a grizzly occasionally gets hold of an odd fawn. Perhaps grizzlies who live far back from the fishing streams don't know about salmon and may hunt mountain goat to fatten on in the fall, and once, high up in the mountains, Jim saw a black bear foolishly chase a mountain goat so far up a precipice that the bear had to inch his way back to safety.

When a grizzly is after food, he has a one-track-mind. Once

Jim heard a grizzly making a tremendous noise in the woods, and sneaked up to watch. The bear was rolling aside huge boulders and sending them down the mountain in an effort to get a mouthful of tiny mice that were hiding in a nest.

He has known them to climb a tree after his deerhide wolf bait. And Ring once saw a morsel of food which had rolled under the porch of the house, and started to lift off the porch to get it. Laurette had to scramble down and pick up the tidbit and give it to her to save the house from destruction.

At a logging camp that moved into the Inlet some years ago, the cook had a little fawn as a pet. When a sow grizzly tried to capture the fawn from his fenced yard, the cook brought his pet into the house. At that, the grizzly first clambered up on the roof; then came down, got her mighty paws between the house and the ground, where blocks supported it against the high tide, and nearly tipped the house over. The loggers ran at her with a big cat tractor, but the grizzly merely sidestepped them and went back to her project. The loggers finally got rifles and shot her, hitched the corpse to the cat tractor and dragged her off to the woods. When her flesh turned to carrion, the other grizzlies ate her.

Jim would never bait for bear. "A grizzly cannot resist carrion," he explains, "and if a guide baits for bear with carrion, he will eventually get every bear that lives in his territory."

But except for its passion for carrion, the grizzly is a wary prey, and Jim soon found that it was one thing to study grizzlies daily in the flats or along his trap line and quite another to lead a strange hunter to the bear. Though the evidence of their recent presence is everywhere—in droppings, tracks, scratches on trees, and in the old animal trails worn down eight inches deep—all the animals miraculously disappear.

Of the much discussed and disputed "blazings" which the grizzlies give their trails, the scratches and bites on certain trees, Jim is inclined to offer a rather undramatic explanation. "Excess energy," he explains. "While they're walking along, feeling good, they reach out and scratch a tree, just as a kid would chuck a stone as he strolls around."

The bear, like the elephant, steps in the same tracks as he moves along an organized trail. A comical sight in the forest is to see a big bear coming along, rolling easily in the spaced tracks which fit his size and bulk; and then to see a little fellow, a cub, behind him, reaching out vainly as he tries to stretch his short legs to fit the oldster's track.

Every well-used bear trail has a "bathtub" every mile or so between the roots of a big spruce or fir tree, where the ground is damp. Here the grizzly digs out a muddy hole, roughly six by eight feet and three or four feet deep. When he is walking along the trail during the summer months and comes to one of these public baths, he crawls in, wallows around a bit, cools off, climbs out, and goes down the trail to the next bath. Where there is no damp earth to dig out, the trails may run five miles between baths. In places with plenty of moisture the bathtubs appear every half-mile.

After many years of watching bears on the move, Jim still has one question for which he has no answer. Repeatedly he has watched the bears travel a trail to a crossing log over a brook, cross over, then jump into the water to swim, fish, or play. Why they do not enter the water where they first come to it, but insist on crossing, Jim cannot understand. To make the mystery deeper, they will pass up endless windfall logs over which they could cross until they come to one particular log, which is apparently labeled "cross log" in their minds.

As the season advances, the grizzlies travel less and less and sleep more and more. They have been gorging all summer, and now they are beginning to slow down. By the last of November the sows have disappeared, and the two-year-olds and old boars turn in a month later, depending on the weather.

19

All God's Creatures

In 1947 Jim became Game Warden for the area, which gives him legal authority to enforce conservation. As more people came into the Inlet and more slaughter occurred, he was determined to stop it, and finally got the job that allows him to. He is also Fire Warden for the Chief Forester, and sees to it that his logging neighbors aren't tempted to keep up their operations when the forests are officially closed because of fire hazard. In a really dry summer, such as that of 1951, when the north wind "feels like a furnace and you can actually see the leaves curling up," close supervision is imperative to avoid the sudden and awful catastrophe of a raging forest fire.

A few years ago the Stantons were offered a good price for their house and land by the Evans Products Company. When they found that they could sell and still retain lifetime interest in their land, with the right to stay on until their deaths, they accepted the offer. Having this backlog in the bank has greatly eased their later years. Now Jim runs his trap line only enough to hold the rights and to keep other trappers from coming into the territory. He takes out hunters in the fall, but there is no longer the constant fight for survival, which meant a year-round heavy schedule of back-breaking work. Both he and Laurette now have time for their beloved animals and birds.

The raccoons come, *en famille,* to eat, but seldom fight over their food. Contrary to popular belief, they do not wash what they eat. Given a clam, they will rinse it because experience has taught them it is sandy, but anything else they simply gobble up, as any other animal does.

Though occasionally a couple will crawl onto the food box outside the front door, and one may push the other off, they usually come one at a time, peer with their curious sharp-chinned faces through the window into the living room, reach a long paw into the box, get their bite, and disappear up to the top of the roof. They love anything sweet: honey, jam, raisins. Laurette has fed them jam from a tablespoon, and once had two of them licking on it at the same time without fighting. When she wants to show off her coon family to visitors, Laurette opens her back door and strews a line of raisins along the floor from the door into the kitchen. The coons walk in, picking up the raisins as they come. Last fall, when Jim was out on his first hunt and Laurette was home alone, she heard a commotion on the porch roof which sounded ominously like a grizzly. She took her flashlight and went out to investigate. It turned out to be Mama, Papa, and four young coons lined up on the porch roof, waiting for a handout. The next morning a hungry bluejay woke her up, pecking at the kitchen window. "Can you beat that!" Laurette said. "Wanting his eats that early—and on Sunday, too!"

The gentle, lovely flying squirrels are a special joy to Laurette. They never fight, and as many as five will eat at once from the feeding shelf by the window. They especially love rolled oats, and dabs of rolled oats and honey bring them in swarms. They are very tame and affectionate, and with them Laurette breaks her rule of handling animals. She picks up the soft, gentle little squirrels, and they cuddle against her throat, like a neckpiece.

The fussy little red squirrels, on the other hand, fight over every morsel among themselves and with every other animal; they are very greedy. One day Laurette heard such scolding that she went out on the woodshed porch—to find a female marten packing away a freshly caught oolichan fish, and a red squirrel complaining shrilly about the theft.

Even mice and rats get special consideration from Laurette. One bob-tailed pack rat, who had lost part of his bushy tail in a fight or accident, chose to take up residence at the Stantons'; this intruder rather upset Laurette's fastidious housekeeping. She wouldn't kill him, but she didn't want him in the house, either. They put him in a covered box and took him up the Franklin River, leaving with him food enough to last until he got back to hunting again, but when they pulled into the home dock, there was the rat down at the beach waiting for them.

Pack rats, by the way, do not "trade" one item for another. They will be carrying one item when something else, shiny or attractive, catches their eye, and they promptly drop whatever they have and pick up the other. It thus appears that they have brought something to trade.

Jim staunchly defends Laurette's inability to kill anything—including rodents. "Animals are company for folks who live in the woods," he says. "They keep us from being lonely. Neither of us will kill these neighbors of ours unless we must."

Scout has now died of old age, and there is nothing to frighten the deer away from the house. When Laurette found that the deer would not eat raw cereals and grain, she baked a special bannock of bran, crushed oats, dairy mash, whole wheat or graham flour, mixed with water. She feeds it not only to the deer but to the marten, squirrels, coons, and birds. Its ingredients are Laurette's chief luxury, costing from seventy to a hundred dollars a season.

"What a woman!" Jim shakes his head sagely. "Imagine!

No Easter bonnets, no trips to town. No new spring outfits. Just more food for her pets!"

Three does come each winter for feed, and six bucks. As the deer have bred, the does have appeared the following season with their fawns. Last winter Laurette fed a dozen deer. This year twenty-three deer showed up. Since the bucks try to hog the food, lifting their front feet to drive off the does, Laurette tries to hand-feed the does and fawns. The Young Doe and Old Doe bring fawns back each year. The Patchy Doe—so named because of her rubbed hide—comes by herself, and has never brought a fawn. Laurette wonders whether the Patchy Doe is barren or if she leaves her fawns in the woods. The buck who keeps his horns on longest, Laurette has found, is always the boss. When he loses his horns, the buck has lost his authority in deer society.

Though one of the does comes on call, and Laurette monitors the feeding each day, she has made no effort to handle the deer or make pets of them. "It would be easy," she explains, "but I don't want to make them dependent on me. If something happened to me, they might go up to someone else —and get killed like our pet grizzly cubs." In summer the deer go off to the hills and feed and aren't seen again till snowtime the following fall.

Though she doesn't handle them, there is no doubt that the deer, squirrels, marten, coons, and birds know very well who feeds them. Laurette never goes to the outhouse, winter or summer, without food in her pockets. In summer the squirrels and birds run after her; in winter the deer spot where she's going, and when she comes out, they form in a ring waiting to surround her.

She feeds all the birds—whisky jacks, bluejays, eagles, grouse, towhees, blackbirds, juncos, chickadees, ducks, geese, and herons.

The "Goofy Duck," which Jim found when he was sawing wood on the beach, was more trouble than all of them. Eight inches long, slate-colored, with yellow legs and a long narrow bill, it was never identified, but Jim brought it home because it was waterlogged. Something had happened so that Goofy could not oil his feathers, and he was so soaked he was unable to fly. Each morning Goofy went down to a little pool on the beach to bathe—and returned soaked. Laurette caught bullheads for him, and Goofy was soon well-fed and happy. He had a crush on Scout, still alive then but growing old and lazy, but it was not reciprocated. When the hound was asleep in front of the fire, Goofy would sneak up and climb onto his back, snuggling down lovingly. When Scout bucked him off and walked away, Goofy trailed happily behind him.

Goofy was a natural-born beggar, and if there was a table of hunters or friends, he went around to each person, working his face and beak, asking for handouts. Picked up in August, Goofy stayed with the Stantons until January when, having recovered from his peculiar affliction, he flew away.

Then there was the twelve-pound wild Canadian goose which Jim found one January day when he went down to his gas-boat. The big gander had been shot through the leg, and the foot which he ordinarily would tuck under his warm wing feathers was stuck out at a helpless angle, frozen. With snow on the ground the goose couldn't get food—nor could Laurette find the proper diet for him. She mixed raw rolled oats with milk, which seemed to do well enough temporarily, and fixed a box for him in the kitchen. The gander would go to bed when they did, sleep until 5 A.M., then climb out of his box and come to wake them up. All geese and ducks must have access to gravel, so Laurette gathered frozen gravel from the beach and thawed it in the oven. "He chonked on it until we almost got nervous prostration!"

Laurette also dug through seven feet of snow to get bits of green grass and roots to augment his oats diet, and served them to him in a pan of water. The gander would pick up the grass in his beak, wash it, then eat it.

While Laurette handled the gander's diet, Jim went to work on his bad leg. At night he would sit by the fire and massage the leg by the hour, gently working it back into usable shape. The gander loved this; he also loved to play with Jim, but he pinched too hard. Jim discovered he could stop him by rubbing his head, which put the gander to sleep.

As his leg improved, the gander tried to learn to fly again. His size kept him from taking off in the kitchen, so he took off from the living room and flew to the kitchen, lighted and ran back to his starting point, and flew one-way again. As those twelve fat pounds hit the air, the carbide lights swung from the ceiling and the pictures clattered against the wall. When a nice warm day finally arrived, Laurette opened the front door. The goose looked outside, came back into the house, then went to the door again and took off, never to return.

A spoonbill duck came up into the yard one day with part of its beak shot away. Jim trimmed the bill so that it could eat, and Laurette fed it clams until it learned to eat with its new-shaped bill.

Having nursed birds suffering the effects of shots that don't kill, it is almost impossible now for Jim to shoot birds, even for food. Last season he went down to the gas-boat to get a dinner's worth of birds, saw the ducks lined up asleep on his boat, and came back empty-handed. An hour later some loggers happened along and shot all of them. The canvasbacks, an almost extinct breed, come and stay in front of the Stantons' house from the first Arctic freeze-up through the winter. Once Jim picked up one which had a ball of ice frozen over its face; it couldn't see or feed. He cracked the ice off its head, fed it a dish of clams, and "you never saw anything gobble up food as fast as that hungry duck!"

During a particularly cold spell Jim found a three-foot-high blue heron on the beach, which was frozen and near death from starvation. He brought it into the house and fed it on red spring salmon. When he put newspapers down in the guest bedroom and kept the heron in there, it promptly climbed up on the bed, saw the mirror, and took up a vigil of narcissistic mirror-gazing, from which even food proved undistracting.

When the bird was fat and well, it went to the front door, as if asking to get out. Two weeks later it walked into the open back door. They fed it a while longer, but when mild weather set in, it left for good.

The wildest of all the birds are the eagles. It took three years to tame one eagle sufficiently to take food from a stick held in their hands. The eagles prey on other birds and animals, forcing kid goats over bluffs by diving on them, then killing them. They try to do the same with young goslings. But the goose and gander fly over their small ones, and with hooks on their wings they nab the eagle as it attempts to dive between them and their young. Contributing to research being done at the University of California, Jim studied eagles and learned that they acquire their bald heads and white tails on their second molting.

Two winters ago some loggers, thinking it amusing, put meat and bones in an open window, encouraging a big male grizzly to come get them. The big bear began coming regularly and got on dangerously familiar terms with the camp and area. One rainy winter night Jim heard a noise and, opening the door, walked right up against the wet hide of the grizzly who was standing in the woodshed with his head and paws on the refrigerator, sniffing for food.

Jim grabbed his rifle, and succeeded in driving the big fellow off without killing him. A few minutes later he heard his caller at the front of the house. The bear was sitting on the front porch. He looked peaceful enough, but a few minutes later Jim heard the sound of something breaking. This time the bear had ripped off the refrigerator door and was lying down on the porch floor with his head poked inside the refrigerator.

Jim decided he would have to kill him. "The first time I was away," he explained, "he might tear down the refrigerator, which runs by oil, and burn the house down. The top of the refrigerator is eight and a half feet high and it had claw marks on it, so you can judge what size he was."

The second time he opened the door, Jim went up to the bear, put the muzzle of the gun against his ear, and started talking to him "real mean." The bear listened a minute, then got to his feet and shuffled off into the woods.

"Next morning," says Jim, "when I went out to see my garden, that fellow had methodically dug up every one of my prize parsnips—as a parting gesture of defiance!"

Jim's worst recent brush with a bear was, oddly enough, a black bear. In July, 1955, Jim and Earl Laughlin, a neighbor and friend who runs the Logco lumber camp on the Franklin River, were making a tour up in the Franklin River country looking at the timber. They were ten miles back in the mountains, four hundred feet up on a tangled mass of slide alder, when they saw a black male bear coming up the slide after them. He was as big as a normal grizzly, about six hundred pounds. The bear came up to within thirty feet of the two men, sized them up, then disappeared through the thick alder. A few minutes later they saw him again, trying to sneak down on them as he would on a mountain goat. They tried to drive him off by yelling at him and throwing rocks, but the bear showed anger, frothing and slobbering as they do when they are working up courage to charge. Jim shot over his head to scare him, but the bear didn't even stop and instead came up to within ten feet of the men. Jim tore off his sharkskin L.L. Bean hunting hat and sailed it into the bear's face to scare him off with human scent.

Instead of being frightened, the bear picked up the hat and ran into the alder. Jim ran after him to retrieve his hat. The bear growled. Jim again shot over his head. The bear dropped the hat and ran a little. Jim snatched up his hat, which had tooth marks bitten through the sharkskin, and ran back out of the alder tangle. He and Earl then went on up the slide for another two hundred yards. But when they climbed on top of a huge boulder the size of a one-story house, they saw the bear still following them. He had sneaked up to within forty feet, slipped into the alders, and again tried to come down on them. Deciding this was one bear that needed the taste of lead, Jim shot him in the fleshy part of the hip, an injury from which he could readily recover. After that warning, the bear shuffled off and quit bothering them.

There was no doubt, however, about the bear's deliberately malicious intent. As the two men went back to their camp-site, they saw tracks that showed the bear had been following them for half a day. When they reached camp, they found that their packsacks, which they had tied thirty feet up in a tree, had been torn down, the food eaten, the dishes chewed, and their sleeping bags and blankets were missing. They finally found the shredded blankets up the mountainside, where the bear had dropped them after dragging them through the woods.

This is the only time in all his years in the woods that a

black bear has given Jim trouble. Knowing that bears hunt mountain goats by sneaking down on them and realizing that they had been hunted in that fashion, Jim thinks the bear may have been old, his eyesight bad, and he figured the men were goats. That, or perhaps he simply connected them with the food in camp.

While Jim is off in the woods, Laurette, alone at home, spends her time cleaning up, washing, bucking up firewood, baking cakes, cookies, and more bread. Although she is alone in the house, she is not afraid of animals. Strange sounds don't bother her: the clatter of coons on the roof or the sly tickle of martens' feet on the outside stair. The only thing she is afraid of is people.

Years ago Jim insisted that she learn to handle a gun for protection. "I taught her," says Jim, "to shoot well enough that she could hit the broadside of a big logger if he came at her." Though now elderly, Laurette's still slender figure and sparkling brown eyes are capable of arousing amorous interest in a lonesome logger, and when Jim is away she opens her door only to old friends, such as the Duncans and until he died, Charlie Panqwit. Charlie died of a throat cancer, and his last words were: "Take me to Chief and Mrs. Kwalate's house. If I drink their good water, my throat will be well."

20

Winter Paradise

The thirty-seven years since they first came into the Inlet in 1919 have made surprisingly few changes in the Stantons' chosen way of life. Today the low, green log house nestles hospitably against the mountain. At one side is a fenced flower garden, filled with red and yellow flowers during the summer months. At the other side is a vegetable garden, with a high wire fence to keep out deer and bear. But they have no electricity, no plumbing, and they still heat their house by wood fire—which they buck up from driftwood into fireplace-size logs down on the beach. Their food order goes in each fall to get them through the winter, and the last steamer touches the Inlet around the first of December, not to return again until the end of March. During this period they have no source of supplies, no telephone, no mail, and little contact with the outside world beyond their battery-driven radio which operates intermittently, depending on weather conditions.

"By the time we get electricity," Jim said, "we'll be too old to snap the switch!"

Their only transportation is the punt and gas-boat with which they run the icy glacial inlet and the turbulent river. Recently a young forest ranger and his friend were caught in a squall and drowned in front of the Stantons' house. In the past five years Jim has three times narrowly escaped under similar conditions, and once stood by his gas-boat, holding it off the rocks for one long stormy night, during which seven scows and five tugboats went under along the coast.

Once a year the Stantons take a run to Alert Bay. There they go on a milk binge, making the rounds of the restaurants and having several glasses of fresh milk at each one. Since they must stay in town overnight, they go to a hotel and enjoy the luxury of eight or ten hot baths during their twenty-four-hour stopover.

Other than fresh milk and hot water, city life has little to offer them. They are both eager to get back home, put the city suit and the wool coat and dress back in mothballs for another year, and get into the slacks and shirts which are their year-round costumes. In midsummer Laurette changes from her winter wool slacks and sweaters to cotton housedresses; Jim simply sheds the extra suit of long cotton underwear which he wears during the winter months. In all her years on the Inlet, Laurette has possessed neither a girdle nor an umbrella, for she has never worried about her weight—still a neat one hundred pounds—or the weather.

Neighbors have made the greatest change in their life. During the winter, a skeleton crew stays on at the three logging camps which now operate in their end of the Inlet; and the young loggers and their wives call on the Stantons regularly for information, help, amusement, and sympathy. Social life is determined by the tide table, which the Stantons keep hanging on a string in their hall, as one might a telephone book. When the tide is right, they can pretty well count on visitors—couples, with and without children and dogs, who drop by unannounced, arriving in their little fiber-glass boats. Whenever the sound of a motor cuts the silent forest air, Jim picks up his binoculars and "puts the glass" to them to see who's coming.

With their long experience and intimate knowledge of the woods, and their warm, hospitable hearts, the Stantons' home is a mecca to all those who locate on the Inlet. The young wives come to Laurette for cooking secrets; for sound advice on how to handle the fresh meat that so often arrives "high" after its journey, what new to do with fish, how to treat wild animals. The men come to Jim to have him help them fix a boat motor; tell them on his maps what channels to take in the rivers, how to get to a glacier or a stream. Mountain climbers, tourists, fishermen, strangers who appear on the Inlet—all check in with Jim for advice and guidance for their projected adventures. Government timber cruisers, wardens, and Evans Products executives stop by on their frequent trips. Whoever comes, no matter what time of night or day, can count on being fed: breakfast, lunch, dinner. In the evening there is hot coffee, homemade bread and jam, homemade cake and ice cream.

A boon to Laurette is the five-year-old Servel coal-oil refrigerator, in which she stores meat, fish, and the gallons of ice cream that Jim loves.

Still an imaginative cook, she has developed a number of recipes to suit the available foods. When they get their deer for the season, which dresses out one hundred to one hundred and thirty pounds of meat, they have a first luxury meal of deer liver and bacon, followed by flavorsome roasts, steaks, and stews.

Laurette learned to smoke fish from the Indians. She also developed her own recipe for fishburgers—chopped raw salmon, seasoned with onion, garlic, and plenty of fresh pepper, then fried in olive oil.

When she dares—which isn't often—Laurette likes to use

190

strong, spicy flavorings, such as chili and curry. But at spices, cheese and cocktail pastes, Jim wrinkles his nose with disgust. "Rotten marten bait" is his brief verdict.

When she can "beat the bears to the cranberries," Laurette cans sauce and catsup, but she always saves out a bunch of the "red snowdrops" to feed the birds through the winter.

Breakfast is the worst meal for her, since she rises tired and without appetite, picking up her usual phenomenal energy after a few cups of scalding black tea. So it is as breakfast cook that Jim shines. He is the official hotcake maker—and his hotcakes, of brown sugar, flour, eggs, cream, and butter, are a special treat. With them he serves country-cut slices of ham, slab bacon, and two or three eggs. It's a feast for the mountain gods, as Jim himself immodestly admits.

Both Stantons are heavy smokers, rolling their own with Players tobacco and papers. One winter during the freeze they ran short of tobacco and began looking around the house for something to smoke. The year before, a policeman friend in Alert Bay had given Laurette a box, which she thought was candy, and the instructions "not to open till she got home." When she opened it, it proved to be a tin of chewing tobacco. Amused, Laurette kept the can, and she and Jim carefully shaved the tobacco into tiny strips and made cigarettes out of it. "One drag," says Laurette, "was enough to knock me out!"

They save up most of their reading material for the winter. Laurette gets to it when she is alone during the fall hunting season. Jim reads later, when the freeze keeps him off his trap line. It is then that he takes "armchair trips all over the world." He has a complete file of the *National Geographic* and, during the frozen-in winter months, he selects a trip and a country he would like to see, then lines up the magazines dealing with that territory, and sets out for a month's voyage on the sea of imagination.

Now in their seventies, Laurette and Jim Stanton will probably end their lives in the forests and the mountains that are home to them and among the animals and birds they have learned to love. But every now and then the bone of contention which they have chewed so often over the years comes up for discussion again.

"Dear," Jim says for the thousandth time, "I've been thinking that we ought to get out of the woods and go back to civilization."

"But Jim," Laurette exclaims, her brown eyes lighting up just as they did when she first said it nearly forty years ago, "this is paradise!"